Pinterest™

FOR DUMMIES®

by Kelby Carr

WILEY

John Wiley & Sons, Inc.

Pinterest™ For Dummies®

Published by
John Wiley & Sons, Inc.
111 River Street
Hoboken, NJ 07030-5774
www.wiley.com

Copyright © 2012 by John Wiley & Sons, Inc., Hoboken, New Jersey

Published by John Wiley & Sons, Inc., Hoboken, New Jersey

Published simultaneously in Canada

For general information on our other products and services, please contact our Customer Care Department within the U.S. at 877-762-2974, outside the U.S. at 317-572-3993, or fax 317-572-4002.

For technical support, please visit www.wiley.com/techsupport.

Wiley publishes in a variety of print and electronic formats and by print-on-demand. Some material included with standard print versions of this book may not be included in e-books or in print-on-demand. If this book refers to media such as a CD or DVD that is not included in the version you purchased, you may download this material at http://booksupport.wiley.com. For more information about Wiley products, visit www.wiley.com.

Library of Congress Control Number: 2012936625

ISBN 978-1-118-32800-2 (pbk); ISBN 978-1-118-35304-2 (ebk); ISBN 978-1-118-35305-9 (ebk); ISBN 978-1-118-37578-5 (ebk)

Manufactured in the United States of America

10 9 8 7 6 5 4 3 2 1

WILEY

About the Author

Kelby Carr is the founder and CEO of Type-A Parent (http://typeaparent.com), a social network and online magazine-style blog founded in 2007 for mom and dad bloggers, and Type-A Parent Conference (http://typeaconference.com), an annual blogging and social media conference founded in 2009 that attracts major corporations and hundreds of parents who blog. She is a social media consultant and speaker.

She's been coding since 1982, social networking online since 1984, web publishing since 1992, blogging since 2002, and tweeting since 2007. She is an early adopter of Pinterest and is active on the site daily with thousands of followers and pins.

Dedication

This book is dedicated to my wonderful husband Mike for his boundless support of this project and every other venture (some sane, some less so) that I pursue. It's also dedicated to my three extraordinary children, who are my motivation and inspiration.

Author's Acknowledgments

So many people helped me write this book that it would be impossible to list everyone. Thank you to the many friends on Twitter, Facebook, and Google+ who so freely offered their thoughts, feedback, and questions about Pinterest, as well as words of encouragement and congratulations. Thank you to everyone on the *For Dummies* team for working with me on this book and making the entire process a pleasant one.

Publisher's Acknowledgments

We're proud of this book; please send us your comments at `http://dummies.custhelp.com`. For other comments, please contact our Customer Care Department within the U.S. at 877-762-2974, outside the U.S. at 317-572-3993, or fax 317-572-4002.

Some of the people who helped bring this book to market include the following:

Acquisitions and Editorial

Project Editor: Blair J. Pottenger

Acquisitions Editor: Amy Fandrei

Copy Editor: Virginia Sanders

Technical Editor: Melanie Nelson

Editorial Manager: Kevin Kirschner

Editorial Assistant: Amanda Graham

Sr. Editorial Assistant: Cherie Case

Cover Photo: © iStockphoto.com / Greg Christman, © iStockphoto.com / Christina J. Stewart, © iStockphoto.com / Sean Locke, © iStockphoto.com / Marjanneke de Jong, © iStockphoto.com / Terry J Alcorn, © iStockphoto.com / Inga Ivanova, © iStockphoto.com / Ruth Black, © iStockphoto.com / Sarah Salmela, © iStockphoto.com / TheCrimsonMonkey, © iStockphoto.com / Hans Martens, © iStockphoto.com / Chee-Onn Leong

Cartoons: Rich Tennant (`www.the5thwave.com`)

Composition Services

Project Coordinator: Patrick Redmond

Layout and Graphics: Claudia Bell, Corrie Niehaus, Lavonne Roberts

Proofreaders: Bryan Coyle, Christine Sabooni

Indexer: Broccoli Information Management

Publishing and Editorial for Technology Dummies

    Richard Swadley, Vice President and Executive Group Publisher

    Andy Cummings, Vice President and Publisher

    Mary Bednarek, Executive Acquisitions Director

    Mary C. Corder, Editorial Director

Publishing for Consumer Dummies

    Kathleen Nebenhaus, Vice President and Executive Publisher

Composition Services

    Debbie Stailey, Director of Composition Services

Table of Contents

Introduction

*P*interest is a mesmerizing and beautiful social network driven by visual content. It's a virtual pinboard, and you can imagine it as an online place where you pin images of things you want to save and remember: quotes that motivate you, do-it-yourself projects you long to do one day, gadgets you would love to buy, pictures from websites that are packed with useful information, or recipes for next Friday's dinner. The primary difference between Pinterest and a physical pinboard hanging over your desk is that your Pinterest pinboards are created and shared with the online world.

Pinterest has been described as an addictive guilty pleasure, but you can find many practical reasons to join Pinterest. It's a powerful platform for organization, planning, and projects. It's a unique way to engage and connect with influential people who have the same interests. It can also be a major traffic generator for websites, blogs, or products. *Real Simple* magazine, in fact, recently told AdAge that Pinterest is beating Facebook when it comes to driving traffic to their site.

Pinterest is new, but it isn't merely a passing fad. The site's growth has been explosive. In January 2011, Pinterest attracted 11.7 million unique visitors, according to comScore. That made it the third fastest-growing website for the month, and the fastest independent site to reach the 10 million monthly unique visitor threshold. The site has received praise in *Time,* which featured it on the 50 Best Websites of 2011 list. It has also been covered in the *Wall Street Journal,* Mashable, and ReadWriteWeb, and it's frequently mentioned in other publications, both online and in print.

About This Book

This book provides all the core instructions you need to jump into Pinterest and thrive. The best way for you to supplement the knowledge you gain in this book is to experience Pinterest hands-on and get comfortable with it.

Pinterest is a site well suited both to early adopters of social media and to newcomers. The platform is simple to use and navigate when you get the hang of it, and this book walks you through all the steps to join, use, socialize, and flourish on Pinterest.

Even though it can seem confusing at first, Pinterest is truly simple when you become familiar with using it. This book is designed to help you get to know your way around, understand all the options and possibilities, and become comfortable on Pinterest. I know that as you dip your toes in, you'll quickly become as captivated by its usefulness and its eye candy as I and millions of others have become.

How This Book Is Organized

This book is organized into chapters that cover everything from snagging a coveted invitation to mastering mobile Pinterest to building a Pinterest following.

If you're brand new to Pinterest, you can read the book from beginning to end as you join the site, create your first pins and boards, and master Pinterest. You can keep this book handy for moments when you get confused, can't find a feature, or need step-by-step instructions to do something in particular.

If you're already a Pinterest member, you can jump right to the chapters that interest you to hone your skills and discover new tips and tricks. Again, you can also keep this book around for times when you have a question or need a walkthrough for a task on Pinterest.

Foolish Assumptions

I'm approaching this book with very few assumptions about your savvy with social media. Experience using popular social networks such as Twitter and Facebook will help. To register for Pinterest, you must be a member of either Twitter or Facebook. Using this book, anyone who's comfortable using the Internet can understand Pinterest.

I do, however, assume that you know how to use a computer and basic online tools such as e-mail and web browsers. If you plan to use Pinterest on a mobile device, I assume you have basic familiarity with your mobile smartphone or tablet. I also assume you have a high comfort level poking around the backend of your site or blog (if you have one) and an understanding of basic web development and HTML to follow all the instructions in Chapter 10.

What I do not assume is your motivation for reading this book. You may want to join Pinterest for entertainment purposes so you can enjoy everything on the site from humor to adorable cat pictures to anything related to *Star Wars* you could possibly dream up. Or you may want to use Pinterest to plan a wedding, a house renovation, or a hot new wardrobe. You might even be pursuing Pinterest mastery for purely business purposes to drive traffic and sales. Any and all of those purposes are perfectly acceptable, and this book helps you accomplish your goals.

Icons Used in This Book

I use some basic icons throughout this book to help you quickly scan and find useful information and tips.

When you see the Tip icon, you're getting a quick tidbit of handy information on using Pinterest.

Some information is important to remember as you use Pinterest, so when you see this Remember icon, be sure to tuck the information away for future reference. Pinterest can be easy to use in mental autopilot mode, so this information is there to help as you navigate the site.

Watch out! As with any social network, you might need to avoid some pitfalls or do a vital task as you participate. Also, because Pinterest is new, I alert you to some need-to-know quirks.

If you love getting a peek at the geek, this icon is for you. Technical Stuff icons alert you when I'm sharing some technical details about Pinterest. If geek just isn't your thing, feel free to skip these — reading them isn't crucial to your understanding and use of Pinterest.

Where to Go from Here

The simplest route is to read this book in order, from beginning to end, but that certainly isn't mandatory. If you're brand new to Pinterest or will be setting up your account as you read this book, I recommend going in order. If you're already on Pinterest and want to understand certain aspects and features better, feel free to jump around to the chapters and sections that interest you. After you read this book, keep it handy as you navigate Pinterest and use it as a reference as needed.

If you get stuck, have a question, or need any help, feel free to ask me! Like and interact with the Facebook Pinterest For Dummies page at www.facebook.com/pinterestfordummies, find me on Twitter at http://twitter.com/typeamom, and, of course, please follow me on Pinterest at http://pinterest.com/kelby. I also have a Pinterest board, Pinterest For Dummies, where I pin helpful articles and resources on Pinterest at http://pinterest.com/kelby/pinterest-for-dummies.

Chapter 1

Getting Started on Pinterest

In This Chapter

▶ Getting and giving an invitation to Pinterest

▶ Creating your Pinterest profile

▶ Finding time to use Pinterest

*P*interest is an online pinboard, a visual take on the social bookmarking site. Unlike other social bookmarking sites, such as Digg and StumbleUpon, content shared on Pinterest is driven entirely by visuals. In fact, you can't share something on Pinterest unless an image is involved.

When you share something on Pinterest, each bookmark is called a *pin*. When you share someone else's pin on Pinterest, it's called a *repin*. You group pins together by topic onto various *boards* or *pinboards* in your profile. Each board mimics a real-life pinboard.

You can share images you find online, or you can directly upload images onto Pinterest. Using the Pin It button (see Chapter 3 for more details), you can share directly in your browser from any web page. You can also share your pins on Twitter and Facebook.

The first time you visit Pinterest, you may notice immediately that it's an aesthetically pleasing site. Figure 1-1 shows the Pinterest home page. You can see how much it relies on visually stunning photos. The second thing you may notice is that you can't join without an invitation. Although I presume the site will eventually become open to public registrations, it's currently in invitation-only mode.

The sections in this chapter walk you through the processes of getting your foot in the door with Pinterest as well as getting your profile set up. At the end, I give you some tips for fitting Pinterest into your busy life.

Figure 1-1: The Pinterest home page.

Joining Pinterest

You have two options for joining Pinterest at the time of this writing:

- ✓ **Request an invitation from Pinterest.** This option requires waiting until your invitation is sent directly from Pinterest. If you choose this option, you should receive an immediate e-mail from Pinterest thanking you for adding your name to the waiting list, and then you must wait for an invitation to arrive. The typical wait time is one to two days, although some have reported waiting as long as two weeks for an invitation.

- ✓ **Ask a friend to invite you.** If you know someone who's a member of Pinterest, ask her to invite you. (She'll need your e-mail address to do so.) The advantage of opting for this method is you get your invitation right away.

I explain both techniques in the following sections. Of course, after you join, one or more of your friends might come calling for an invitation, or you might just feel like spreading your love of Pinterest, so I also explain how to send invitations.

To sign up, you must either register via your Facebook account or your Twitter account. One or the other is required to sign up for Pinterest.

Requesting an invitation from Pinterest

Requesting an invitation is quite simple — just follow these steps:

1. **Click the large, red Request an Invite button on the top-middle area on the Pinterest home page. (Refer to Figure 1-1.)**

   A form appears, as shown in Figure 1-2.

   Enter your e-mail address here...

   then click this button

   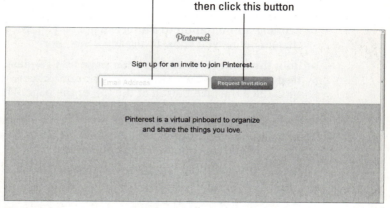

Figure 1-2: Enter your e-mail address to request an invite.

2. **Enter your e-mail address and click the Request Invitation button, as shown in Figure 1-2.**

   Now you just have to wait for Pinterest to send you an invite. You'll receive a confirmation e-mail letting you know you're on the wait list. Eventually, a formal invitation will arrive in your inbox in about one to two days.

   If you don't receive the confirmation e-mail within minutes, check your e-mail's spam folder. If the confirmation e-mail goes into spam, the chances are good the actual invitation will land in the spam folder as well, and you'll miss it. If the confirmation e-mail did land there, use your e-mail provider's method for reporting that an e-mail is not spam.

Asking a member for an invitation

The quicker and easier method of getting an invitation is to ask for one from a friend who's already a Pinterest member. The great advantage to this method is that you get instant gratification because you receive your invite immediately (rather than being on the wait list). The disadvantage is that you need to know someone who is a Pinterest member. That might not be as difficult as you think, however. Pinterest has 4 million users (and that number is growing rapidly), and many members are happy to help newcomers join.

Here are a few ways to find a friend to ask to invite you:

- ✔ **Post a status update on Twitter or Facebook that you're seeking an invitation to Pinterest.** In many cases, you'll find that someone you know is already a member.

- ✔ **Join the Pinterest Facebook fan page and request an invitation from fellow fans.** Go to www.facebook.com/pinterest. Click the Like button at the top of the page. Then write a post on the wall requesting an invitation and be sure to include your e-mail address. (However, don't use this method if you're not comfortable posting your e-mail address, or use an e-mail address you don't mind posting.)

- ✔ **Search Pinterest on Twitter to see whether someone you know is a member already.** To do so, log in to Twitter and enter **Pinterest** as a search term in the top Search bar or visit http://twitter.com/#!/search/pinterest. The search results include anyone who has shared a pin on Twitter in a tweet as well as people who tweet about Pinterest.

- ✔ **Browse Pinterest.com to see whether someone already there is a friend of yours.** You can either visit the home page pins to see whether you recognize any names (a long shot) or type a name into the Search field in the top-left corner of the screen. When you get the results, click People to view search results by users' names.

- ✔ **Post on other social networks, such as Google+, to see whether someone is a member of Pinterest.**

- ✔ **Check the Pinterest page on Facebook.** Go to www.facebook.com/pinterest and click the Like button if you haven't already. You see a list of your friends who are Pinterest fans (as shown in the top right of Figure 1-3). From there, you can message a friend (either through Facebook's private messaging on your friend's profile page or, if you know it, through the person's e-mail address) and ask for an invitation.

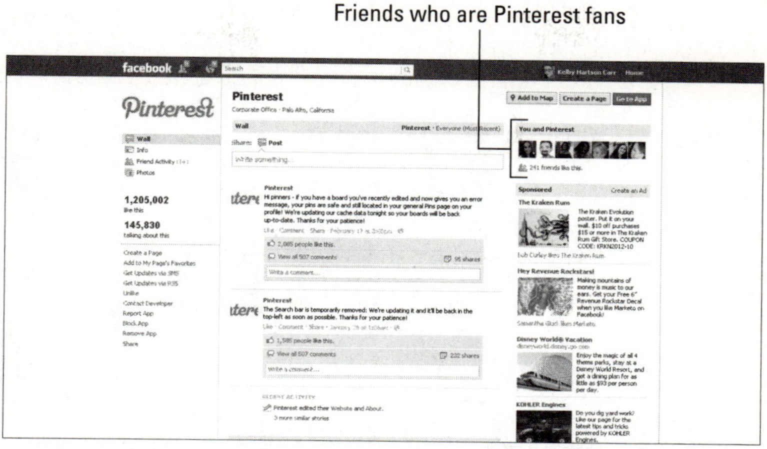

Friends who are Pinterest fans

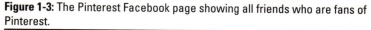

Figure 1-3: The Pinterest Facebook page showing all friends who are fans of Pinterest.

When you've found a friend who is willing to invite you to Pinterest, give that friend your e-mail address. Then your friend can formally invite you to join Pinterest using the methods I describe in the section "Integrating Pinterest with your Facebook or Twitter account."

Inviting a friend to join Pinterest

When your friends see how much fun you're having with Pinterest, they might want in on the action. You can formally invite a friend to join Pinterest by logging into your Pinterest account and choosing any one of these three methods:

✔ Click the Invite Now button in the top-right corner of the Pinterest home page. (See Figure 1-4.)

✔ Mouse over your name in the top-right corner of the Pinterest home page and choose the Invite Friends option from the drop-down menu.

✔ Mouse over your name in the top-right corner of the Pinterest home page and choose Find Friends from the drop-down menu. A new page appears listing Facebook friends you can invite and listing your Facebook friends who are already using Pinterest. From here, you can click the red Invite Friends button on the left side. Note that if you click the main Invite Friends button, all people will be sent an invitation (which could annoy them). Alternatively, you can click each name individually to hand-pick which friends you invite.

Click this button

Figure 1-4: Invite Friends button on Pinterest.

Integrating Pinterest with your Facebook or Twitter account

After you receive your invitation, you're all set, right? Well, maybe. To register, you must first have a Twitter or a Facebook account. Although this might appear to be an inconvenience, restricting registrations to those already active in social media seems to have had the desired effect of preventing spam submissions on Pinterest.

To integrate your Facebook or Twitter account with Pinterest, follow these steps:

1. Get a Facebook or Twitter account.

   If you don't already have a Twitter (http://twitter.com) or a Facebook (www.facebook.com) account, you need to create one. You can get an account for free with either one, and you can set up an account with either very easily and quickly. You also need to activate the account or accounts before you can use them for your Pinterest registration.

   If you must choose only one social network to integrate, note that Facebook has the advantage of pulling in all friends on that network to allow you to easily add them as friends on Pinterest.

2. **Log in to your Facebook or Twitter account.**

   Logging in isn't strictly necessary at this point, but doing so makes your registration go more smoothly.

3. **In the Pinterest invitation e-mail you received, click the link to register.**

   The Pinterest registration screen appears, as shown in Figure 1-5.

Pinterest

Congratulations! You've been invited to join Pinterest.

Sign Up with Facebook f We NEVER post without your permission

Or sign up with **Twitter**. **Why link accounts?**

Figure 1-5: The Pinterest registration screen asks you sign up via Facebook or Twitter.

4. **Click either the Facebook button or the Twitter link.**

   If you're a member of both, Facebook is preferable because you'll see the option to add friends from that network. However, you can add either one at registration and then integrate the other one later if you choose.

5. **Enter your profile details in the text boxes provided.**

   You're prompted for three basic profile details, as shown in Figure 1-6:

   • Your username

   • Your e-mail address

   • Your password

Choose your username carefully. It determines the URL for your profile on Pinterest. (For example, mine is `http://www.pinterest.com/kelby`.) Pinterest recently added the option to change your username — however, it's not ideal to do so because any links to your profile will no longer work.

If you're creating a Pinterest business account, you might want to use your company's name in your profile instead of your personal name.

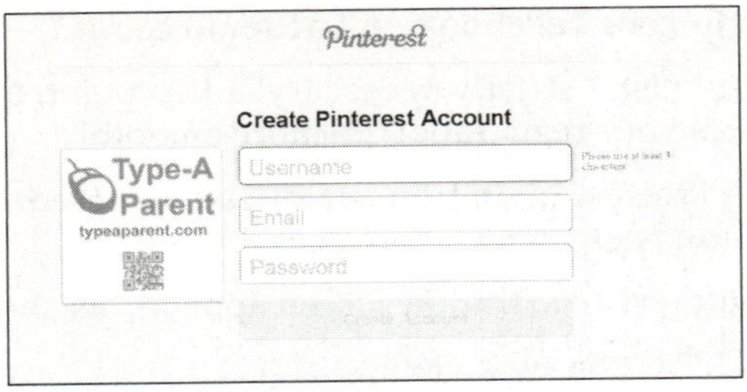

Create Pinterest Account

Username

Email

Password

Figure 1-6: Create your Pinterest profile.

After you fill out this information, you're officially a member of Pinterest — congratulations! Continue reading the next section to find out how to complete the setup of your new Pinterest profile.

Setting Up Your Profile

After you've integrated Pinterest with your Facebook or Twitter account (see the previous section), you must go through a few steps to set up your basic Pinterest profile. This profile takes only a few seconds to complete. When you're finished, you'll be following some Pinterest members, and you'll see pins in your stream.

Some of these options appear only during the registration process (such as the suggested followers), so be aware you won't be able to return to all of these steps. To begin setting up your profile, follow these steps:

1. **Indicate your interests by clicking the images for any that apply.**

    Figure 1-7 shows the Interests page with a few items already selected.

    Although Pinterest tells you it's going to suggest a few members for you to follow, this statement is a little misleading. In actuality, Pinterest automatically sets up your account to follow a few members who match your interests. (If you don't want to follow these members, no problem — you can unfollow them right away as I describe in the next step.)

2. **Click the Follow People button at the bottom of the page (you may need to scroll down to view the button).**

Figure 1-7: Choose interests during profile set up.

3. **Review the members you're now following and make any necessary adjustments.**

   After you indicate your interests, Pinterest displays the list of members it has chosen for you to follow. (See Figure 1-8.) Pinterest also automatically sets up your profile to follow those friends from either Twitter or Facebook (whichever you used to register) who are already established on Pinterest. At this stage, you can click the Unfollow button to remove anyone you don't want to follow from this list.

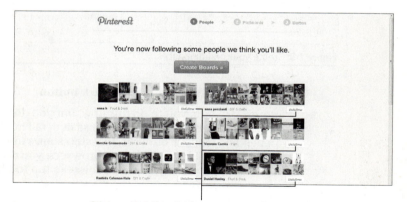

Click an Unfollow button to remove that person

Figure 1-8: See who Pinterest followed for your profile.

4. **Create your first pinboards by clicking the Create Boards button. (Refer to Figure 1-8.)**

5. On the screen that appears (see Figure 1-9), name your new pinboards by using the appropriate text boxes.

Your profile and pins will be organized by these boards. Pinterest automatically suggests some boards for you to create, such as Products I Love, Favorite Spaces and Places, and Books Worth Reading. You can use those, or you can change the text in the boxes to boards you would like to create. To delete a suggested board, mouse over the right side of the box. Click the *x* that appears in the bottom-right corner of any board name to remove that board.

You don't need to agonize over boards as you go through this process. You can easily create more boards later. (I cover creating boards in detail in Chapter 2.) You can also edit the name and description of a board at any time.

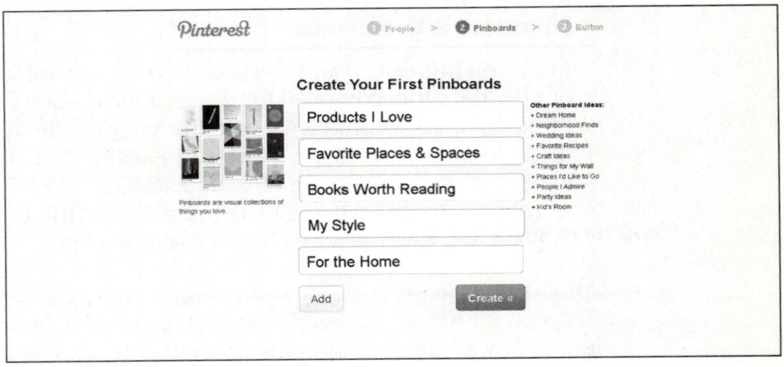

Create Your First Pinboards

Products I Love

Favorite Places & Spaces

Books Worth Reading

My Style

For the Home

Add   Create

Other Pinboard Ideas:
+ Dream Home
+ Neighborhood Finds
+ Wedding Ideas
+ Favorite Recipes
+ Craft Ideas
+ Things for My Wall
+ Places I'd Like to Go
+ People I Admire
+ Party Ideas
+ Kid's Room

Pinboards are visual collections of things you love.

Figure 1-9: Create your first pinboards.

---

6. (Optional) Add the Pin It bookmark button.

Pinterest prompts you to do this now, but you don't have to. You can wait until I cover this process in detail in Chapter 3. Depending on your browser, this step shows instructions on adding a Pin It button. In most browsers, you drag the button on the screen up to your browser's top toolbar.

Adding a profile picture

When you signed up, Pinterest acquired your default profile image automatically — it copied the profile image you were using at the social network that you integrated during registration. If you'd like, you can change that image at any time.

To change your profile picture, log in to Pinterest, mouse over your name in the top-right corner of the Pinterest home page, and choose Settings from the drop-down menu. When the Settings page appears, scroll down a bit to see your Image options, as shown in Figure 1-10.

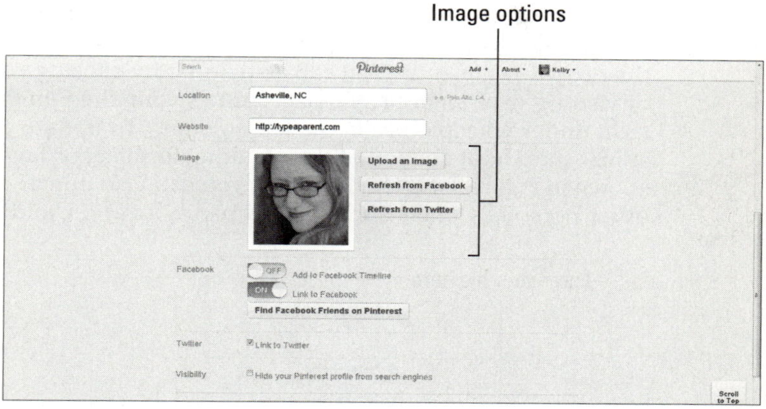

Image options

Figure 1-10: Update your profile picture.

You have three choices:

- ✔ **Upload an Image:** To upload an image from your computer, click this button. The button changes instantly to a text field and a Browse button. Click the Browse button to open the Choose File to Upload dialog box. Then navigate through your files to seek out your image, select it, and click the Open button to upload it to Pinterest.

- ✔ **Refresh from Facebook:** If you have an updated image from Facebook you would like to use, click this button. This option appears only if you have Facebook integrated with your Pinterest account.

- ✔ **Refresh from Twitter:** Like the Facebook button, this button changes your profile image to the one you're currently using on Twitter. This option appears only if you have Twitter integrated with your Pinterest account.

An ideal profile image is square. Also, it must at least be 200 x 200 pixels in size, or it will appear pixelated and distorted on your profile page.

Adding a bio

A bio helps tell others on Pinterest about you. When someone
visits your profile page, your bio is displayed just below your
profile picture in the left column.

To update your bio, log in to Pinterest, mouse over your name in
the top-right corner of the home page, and choose Settings from
the drop-down menu. (You can also find it by clicking your name
or visiting your main profile page and clicking the Edit Profile link
right under your picture in the left column.) To update your bio,
adjust the About section of the resulting form accordingly, as
shown in Figure 1-11. On this form, you can also update various
other personal details such as your name, location, and website.

Enter your bio here

Notifications	**Change Email Settings**
Password	**Change Password**
First name	Kelby
Last name	Carr
Username	kelby
About	Kelby Carr is the founder and publisher of Type-A Parent. She also is the organizer of the Type-A Parent Conference. You can follow her on Twitter at @typeamom.
Location	Asheville, NC
Website	http://typeaparent.com
Image	Upload an Image

Figure 1-11: Enter your bio on Pinterest.

 The bio is text only. You can't use HTML coding in your bio to, say,
place sections in boldface or to add a link to your site. Any HTML
code will be displayed, not rendered, and if you include a full URL,
it won't be made into a clickable link. You can, however, include a
linkable web page or blog URL in the Website field in Settings. (See
Figure 1-11.)

Setting your e-mail preferences

Do you want Pinterest to notify you of all activity related to your
profile by e-mail alert? Or do you dislike e-mails and prefer to
get your updates when you go directly to the site? The Pinterest

settings allow for a variety of preferences. Figure 1-12 shows a list of options you can choose to refine your updates; you access this list by clicking Settings and then selecting Email Preferences.

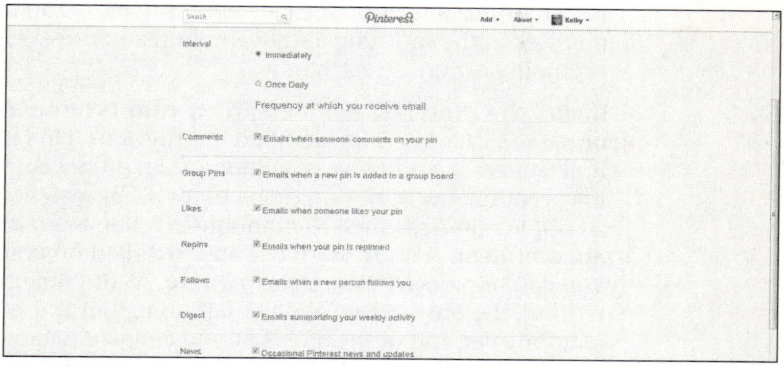

Figure 1-12: E-mail preferences in Pinterest.

E-mail alerts are handy for keeping track of activity, such as when people repin (or share) your pins, follow you, or comment on your pins. At the time of this writing, though, the e-mail sends are spotty. Pinterest is a new site, and glitches are to be expected. Don't rely only on e-mail notifications — check Pinterest as well. To access this information at Pinterest, mouse over your name and choose Pins from the drop-down menu to see the number of repins, likes, and comments for your latest pins. Pinterest also shows the latest activity in the left column on the home page when you're logged in. For more detail on a particular pin, click its thumbnail to navigate to the pin page.

Finding Time for Pinterest

Pinterest can be addictive when you get the hang of it. That can be great if you have all the time in the world. However, because I don't have all the time in the world, I've discovered many ways to be active and engaged on Pinterest without letting it get in the way of work, life, sleep, and other social networks. Here are a few tips:

 ✔ **Have dedicated Pinterest time each day for pinning, repinning, liking, and commenting.** For example, I find it can be a nice way to start the morning over coffee when I'm gearing up for doing work. You don't need to make it one time a day, because you can make pins in rapid-fire fashion, spending five minutes here and five minutes there.

✔ **Limit it to a certain number of minutes.** For a heavy user with many boards to maintain, this could mean 10–15-minute stretches three or four times a day for pinning and repinning, creating and populating new boards, and liking and commenting on other pins. For a new or lighter user, it could mean five minutes in the morning and five minutes in the evening of repinning others' great pins.

✔ **Install the Pinterest mobile app on your iPhone if you have one.** (See Chapter 7 for detailed instructions.) In fact, I use Pinterest more often on my iPhone than on my computer. It's great for those boring times in life when you need to kill a couple minutes, such as standing in a line or waiting for an appointment to start. With the app installed on your phone, you can hop onto Pinterest anywhere. At the time of this writing, the only native app is on iPhone, but there is also a mobile version of the site that you can use on any touch-screen phone or tablet.

✔ **Schedule your time wisely.** Allow for more time on Pinterest when you first begin. The extra time will help you get the hang of the site and get comfortable. Make plans to scale the time back as you grow comfortable with the site and build a core of followers.

Chapter 2

Creating Boards

*W*hen you sign up for Pinterest (see Chapter 1), you're given the option to automatically add some boards based on suggestions from Pinterest. Creating your first board is easy, and now you have time to put some thought into it.

Boards are the main organization system for Pinterest and are designed to be a simulation of a pinboard hanging up on your wall. It might help to think of boards as buckets with labels on them. Boards organize your pins into a variety of topics, and you get to create those topics. For instance, Figure 2-1 shows my Geeky Goodness board, where I collect articles and pictures that appeal to my geek side.

Figure 2-1: An example Pinterest board.

Health Care Art

Lighthouses
Primitive (Nostalgia)
Cape Cod Travel
Recipes
Art that Inspires Me

20   Pinterest For Dummies

Picking a Topic

Before you create a new board, consider what interests you have that others might have as well. By creating boards that cover interests that others share, you can encourages people to follow you or your boards and engage with those who share your interests. You can be general, or you can be specific, but it should be an interest that will have content worth pinning. Pinterest has become known for certain genres of content (such as food and crafts), but you need not limit yourself to traditionally pretty or artistic topics.

For example, *Star Wars* and *Harry Potter* are wildly popular topics. Some boards are general, such as business and travel. For example, I have a board that's simply called "red." Some boards are extremely specific, such as Mason jars and paint chip crafts.

A board with just a pin or two isn't very appealing, so before you create a board be sure you're interested enough in the topic to populate it with pins.

When creating boards, you need not limit yourself to personal interests. You can also get creative and use boards for business purposes. You can create a board of ideas for work projects, or you can use a board to creatively promote topics of interest to your readers or customers if you have a blog or a business. For example, if you have a gaming blog, you can create a board of your favorite games; if you sell jewelry, you can create a board of colors or images in nature that inspire your work.

Creating Your First Board

To create a new board on Pinterest, follow these steps:

1. **Sign in to your Pinterest account and click the Add+ button in the top-right corner of the Pinterest home page.**

   The Add dialog box appears and presents you with three choices: Add a Pin, Upload a Pin, and Create a Board. (See Figure 2-2.)

2. **Click the Create a Board option.**

3. **When prompted, enter the basic information about your board: the name, category, and who can pin on this board. (See Figure 2-3.)**

   Check out the following sections for more information on naming, categorizing, and deciding who can contribute to your board.

Click this option

Figure 2-2: The Add dialog box lets you add pins or create a new board.

Figure 2-3: Choose a board name, category, and contributors for your new board.

As you're creating a board, it doesn't have a spot for a description. After you create your board, click the Edit Board button in the top-middle of your board and add a description. This isn't necessary, but it does appear at the top of the page when someone visits your board. You can also find out more about editing your board later in this chapter.

Naming your board

Pinterest is a unique animal on the Internet. In most cases online, being straightforward and clear is ideal. Because creativity is so prevalent on Pinterest, consider mixing boards that have unique and clever names with others that have basic, plain names.

For example, I have a board of craft and DIY projects. I could have named it that, but instead I named it "Stuff I Will Never Get Around to Making." My board related to children is "For the Short People." Although you won't always have inspiration to get clever, when you can it's more engaging. The trick is to be both clever and clear so people understand what they can find on the board.

You can always go back and change it later. Keep in mind, however, that after you name a board, it sets the URL for the board. If you later change it, the URL will also change (and any links to the board directly will no longer work). Check out the "Editing Your Boards" section, later in this chapter, to find out how to rename your board.

You can have the same board name as other users because the final URL for your board will include your username (in a format of pinterest.com/USERNAME/BOARDNAME).

Board names have a 180-character limit, so you have to keep it brief. Also, the board name can get cut short in some instances, such as on your profile page. Avoid using any more than seven words.

Choosing a category

Pinterest allows people to browse by category, so be sure to choose a category that accurately describes your board.

In most instances, identifying a category for your board is pretty clear. Pinterest has several categories that cover a wide variety of topics. Click the down-pointing arrow on the right end of the Board Category field (refer to Figure 2-3) and use the drop-down menu to choose the one that best fits. Again, you can change this later. (See the "Editing Your Boards" section, later in this chapter, to find out how.)

You're limited to the category options Pinterest makes available. Unfortunately, some boards don't categorize well. If that's the case for your board, find the best fit (or something general, such as My Life) and move on — don't let it stop you from creating a board that's a good idea.

Picking a category can be tricky at times, especially if you have a board that would fall nicely into two different categories. In some instances, it's a judgment call on your part as to which is best. If you're torn, you can also look at other pins in the categories you're considering to help determine which is the better fit.

Deciding who can contribute to your board

You can create a board that only you can pin to, or you can create a board that allows other Pinterest users to contribute to it. In most situations, especially if you're new to Pinterest, a solo board (where only you can add items) makes the most sense. To create a board that only you can pin to, select the Just Me option next to the Who Can Pin? question. (Refer to Figure 2-3.)

Searchability versus creativity

Being creative when naming your Pinterest boards is counter to search engine optimization best practices (and I'm seeing Pinterest boards appear frequently in Google search results). This is something for you to note and to consider. Still, I would argue that Pinterest is a place to showcase your creativity. I believe you'll have more impact by being interesting in Pinterest than by ranking higher in Google search results. I recommend having a combination of boards with creative names and boards with straightforward names to gain the benefits of both creativity on Pinterest and search engine rankings.

On the other hand, a group board offers many interesting possibilities, such as the following:

- ✔ Collaborating on work projects, such as sharing articles that offer tips on a specific industry or case studies that are relevant to the staff

- ✔ Planning a home renovation with your family and contractors, sharing things such as color schemes, sample rooms, DIY project articles, and room layouts that you like

- ✔ Promoting a joint cause or topic, sharing content that is relevant such as statistics on the issue, ways to donate or volunteer, and stories of people helped by the cause

- ✔ Sharing seasonal or topical content, such as a holiday cookie board to collect and share recipes or a Mother's Day board to share crafts for kids to make gifts

To create a group board, select the Me + Contributors option. (See Figure 2-4.) You can add members either by their Pinterest member name or their e-mail address. Figure 2-4 shows what happens if you start typing a member name in the text box: Pinterest automatically populates a list of possible matches, and you can select the right person from the list. Then just click the Add button next to the name.

To invite someone via e-mail, type or paste in e-mail addresses one at a time in the field that appears when you click Me + Contributors and then click Add.

Some people don't like to be added to boards without being asked first, especially because the boards then appear on their own profiles. When in doubt, it's best to check with people first before you add them to a group board.

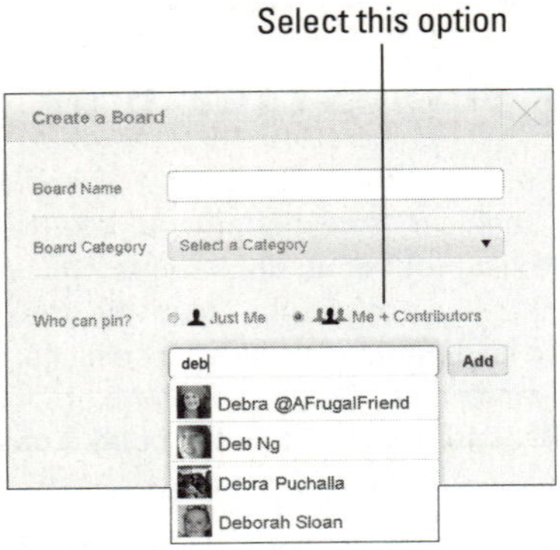

Select this option

Create a Board ✕

Board Name

Board Category   Select a Category   ▼

Who can pin?   ○ 👤 Just Me   ● 👥 Me + Contributors

deb| Add

👤 Debra @AFrugalFriend

👤 Deb Ng

👤 Debra Puchalla

👤 Deborah Sloan

Figure 2-4: You can add contributors to a board.

Rearranging Your Boards

After you create some boards, you may want to rearrange them to bring your favorite and most well-pinned boards to the top. To rearrange your boards, follow these instructions:

1. **Go to your profile page by clicking your name in the top-right corner of the screen.**

2. **Click the Rearrange Boards icon (which looks like a computer screen with two arrows) under your name and bio in the center of the screen directly to the right of the words Edit Profile.**

3. **Click and hold on a board to move it, then release the mouse button when you have the board where you want it.**

   Figure 2-5 shows how to drag and drop a board to a new position.

4. **Click the Save Arrangement button.**

Figure 2-5: Rearrange your boards by dragging and dropping.

Editing Your Boards

At some point, you might want to edit one or more of your boards for various reasons. Maybe you came up with a better name for the board, or perhaps you want to add a description. It could be that Pinterest added new categories, and one is a better fit. Whatever the reason, fortunately it's easy for you to change the details of your boards at any time.

Be aware that changing the name of a board also changes its web URL. If you or anyone else has linked to your board, using the old link they will get an error. For example, `pinterest.com/yourname/yourboard` becomes `pinterest.com/yourname/newboardname`. Any links to the board from outside Pinterest should be updated with the new URL. If someone besides you has linked to it, there's likely little you can do to correct that (except approach each person who linked and ask), so those links will be dead.

To edit a board, follow these steps:

1. **Visit your profile by clicking your name in the top-right corner of the screen.**

2. **On your profile page, find the board that's in need of some editing attention. Click the Edit button for that board.**

    The Edit Board screen appears, as shown in Figure 2-6.

3. **Change the title, description, who can pin on the board, and/or the category.**

4. **When you're done making changes, click the Save Settings button.**

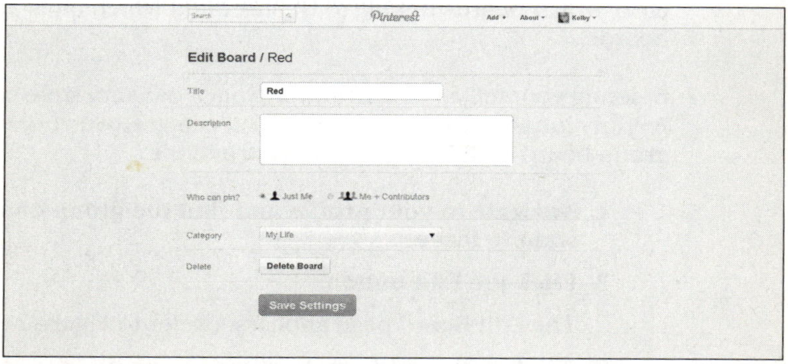

![Edit Board screen showing fields for Title, Description, Who can pin, Category, and a Delete Board button with Save Settings button]

Figure 2-6: You can edit your board as needed.

Deleting a Board

In most instances, you edit a board if there's something about it you don't like. Still, sometimes boards don't make sense anymore. The boards you created when Pinterest prompted you at log in might need the old heave ho, for example. Or you might have two boards that overlap in content.

If you want to delete a board because another one is too similar, you might consider first repinning the pins from the board about to be deleted onto the one that will remain. Otherwise, all your pins on the board about to be deleted will be gone.

If you need to delete a board, follow these steps:

1. **On your profile, find the board you want to delete.**

2. **Click the Edit button on the board.**

   The Edit Board page appears. (Refer to Figure 2-6.)

3. **Click the Delete Board button and confirm.**

Leaving a Collaborative Board

You may find that people add you to collaborative boards that you don't want to participate in. Some might be too marketing-oriented, or it might be a topic that doesn't interest you. Because people can add you to a board (as long as you follow one another) without your approval, this can be an issue. Also, after you're added to someone else's group board, the board appears on your own profile. At immediate glance on a profile's pinboards, it isn't clear which boards belong to the user and which ones are group boards.

Deleting yourself as a contributor from a collaborative board isn't terribly intuitive, but it is simple. You can remove yourself from a group board by following these instructions:

1. **Navigate to your profile and find the group board you want to leave.**

2. **Click the Edit button.**

   The Edit Board page appears. (Refer to Figure 2-6.)

3. **Scroll down until you find your name on the list of pinners for that board, as shown in Figure 2-7.**

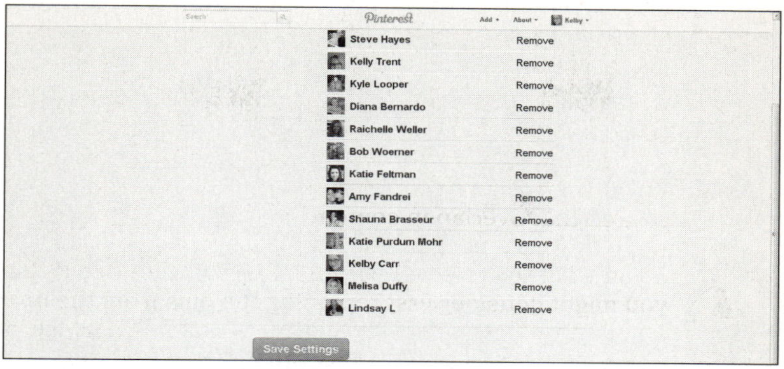

Search | Pinterest | Add ▾ About ▾ Kelby ▾

Steve Hayes		Remove
Kelly Trent		Remove
Kyle Looper		Remove
Diana Bernardo		Remove
Raichelle Weller		Remove
Bob Woerner		Remove
Katie Feltman		Remove
Amy Fandrei		Remove
Shauna Brasseur		Remove
Katie Purdum Mohr		Remove
Kelby Carr		Remove
Melisa Duffy		Remove
Lindsay L		Remove

Save Settings

Figure 2-7: You can remove your profile from a group board.

4. **Click Remove to the right of your name.**

   You're removed from the board and can no longer pin items to it.

If you created the board, you cannot remove yourself from it. You see only the option to remove members you added or delete the board.

Chapter 3

Pinning and Repinning

*T*he true life of Pinterest is in the pins. Pins represent a wide variety of subjects, but they all have one thing in common: They all involve an image or a video. (See Figure 3-1.) This is one way in which Pinterest is unique as a social bookmarking site. Most social bookmarking sites are driven by words, and they might allow images or video as an afterthought. On Pinterest, however, the visuals drive the site.

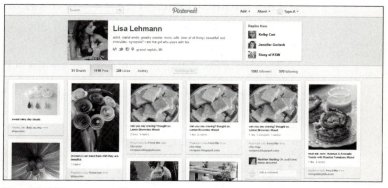

Figure 3-1: Pins on a profile.

Creating Your First Pin

A pin can be anything visual. Pins that are eye-catching, beautiful, unique, funny, or interesting get pinned most frequently. If you want to share or save an image or a video of something, pinning it is a great way to do so.

Adding a pin with a website URL

When you find a web page that you know you'll want to return to, then as long as the page has an image for pinning, you can follow a few simple steps to pin it by using the web page's URL.

Unless you have a compelling reason, don't pin from the home page for a site. Particularly on a blog, an image from a post will move off the home page, and later on, people won't be able to find the source. If you see a post on a blog home page, click the title to go to the *permalink* (the longer, deep link that takes a reader directly to a post instead of the list of posts on the home page) for that post and use that URL.

When you find an image you want to pin — whether it's in a recipe, an article, or something else — follow these instructions to pin it to your board:

1. **Copy and paste the URL of the page where the image appears.**

   You do this by going to the page where the image is located. In your browser's address bar, click and highlight the entire URL. Then copy that address.

2. **Use your web browser to navigate to** http://pinterest.com **and log in.**

3. **Click the Add + button at the top-right corner of the screen.**

   The Add dialog box appears.

4. **Click the Add a Pin button.**

   The Add a Pin dialog box appears, as shown in Figure 3-2.

Paste the URL here

Add a Pin	
http://	Find Images

Figure 3-2: Paste the URL.

5. **Paste the URL you copied in Step 1 into the URL field in the Add a Pin Window.**

6. **Click the Find Images button.**

   The Add a Pin dialog box expands to show these additional options (see Figure 3-3):

   • Images from the page

   • A drop-down list of your boards

   • A description text box

Images from the page   Drop-down list of your boards

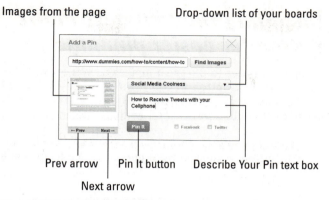

Prev arrow   Pin It button   Describe Your Pin text box

Next arrow

Figure 3-3: Add a pin with a URL.

7. **To choose an image from the page, click the Next or Prev arrow (refer to Figure 3-3) until you find the image you would like to pin.**

   You can select only one image at a time from the page.

8. **Use the drop-down list of your boards to select the board for the pin.**

   If none of your boards suit this new pin, you can create a new board, as I explain in the later section, "Creating a new board on the fly."

9. **Type a description of the pin in the Describe Your Pin text box.**

   It can be easy to forget that viewers of your pin will have no context for the image. They won't see the title of the source web page that it came from. Be sure to not only use the description to say how you feel about what you're pinning (such as "great tips") but to clearly say exactly what it is (such as "great tips on receiving tweets on your cellphone"). You can also have fun with the description to make it more engaging, to add your personality stamp to it, and to give your followers a sense of why you pinned it.

10. **Click the Pin It button.**

    You're taken directly to your pin's page.

If you add a pin from a website, you don't need to provide a source in the description. Pinterest automatically links the image and the pin to the original URL you provided, and it shows the main domain name of the website on the pin's page.

Installing the Pinterest Pin It button for easier pinning

To make it easier to pin great images as you browse the Internet, install the Pin It button to your web browser toolbar. When it's installed, you can click the Pin It button from any web page. To install the Pin It button, follow these steps:

1. **Log in to your Pinterest account and click the About button in the top-right corner of the Pinterest home page.**

   A menu appears.

2. **Choose Pin It Button from the menu.**

   The Pinterest Goodies page appears.

3. **Scroll to the top of the Goodies page to find the Pin It button, as shown in Figure 3-4.**

   Pinterest can tell which browser you're using and provides browser-specific instructions for installing the Pin It button.

4. **Follow the instructions on Pinterest for installing the Pin It button in your particular browser.**

   The steps can vary slightly from browser to browser. Most instructions involve dragging the Pin It button image onto the bookmark toolbar at the top of your browser window.

Pinterest provides a video on how to install the Pin It button. If you don't see the video right away, scroll down a little bit on the page.

Pin It button

Table 3-4: The Pin It button and instructions.

Using the Pin It button to add a pin

The Pin It button makes it quick and easy to pin images during your normal web browsing. Instead of copying and pasting URLs and going between Pinterest and the site you're browsing, you can do it all in a couple of clicks. You need not even leave the site you're browsing.

1. **Navigate to the page with the image you'd like to pin to a board.**

   You should already be logged in to Pinterest.

2. **Click the Pinterest Pin It button on your bookmark toolbar, shown in Figure 3-5.**

   A new page appears showing any pinnable images from the page. (See Figure 3-6.) Below each image are the dimensions of the image in pixels.

   Keep in mind that larger images look better on Pinterest than smaller ones. Also be aware that some images simply can't be pinned due to the coding, and also because Pinterest allows sites to opt out of being pinned. If either is the case, you can't pin those images.

3. **Click the image you want to pin.**

   The Create Pin pop-up window appears.

Pin It button on toolbar

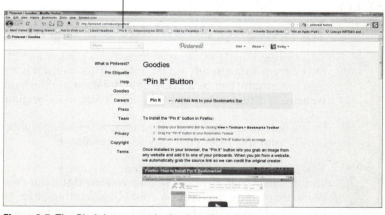

Figure 3-5: The Pin It button on the bookmark toolbar.

Pinnable images

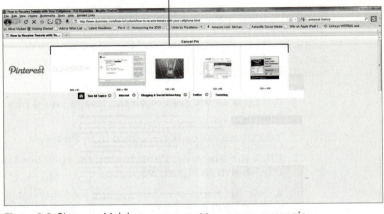

Figure 3-6: Choose which image you want to appear as your pin.

4. **Use the drop-down list to select the board you want to pin to. Then type a description.**

   What if you don't yet have a board that this new pin belongs on? You can create a new board by following the steps in the later section, "Creating a new board on the fly."

5. **Click the Pin It button.**

   You then see a dialog box that gives you the option to view your pin or (if you have Twitter integrated) tweet your pin.

Uploading an image as a pin

You can also upload your own image as a pin instead of having to pin content that already exists online. This method is handy but also potentially can be a copyright violation. Unlike a pin from a website, a direct image upload doesn't link to its original source.

Image upload can be great for pinning interesting sights you see during your day or in your travels, for example.

You should upload only images that you take yourself, and you should make that clear in the way you word the pin description. For example, the description could be something like, "We're in Paris! Here's a picture I took of the Eiffel Tower." Uploading other people's images can be a copyright violation because they own the rights to the image, particularly if you don't link to the source and add a photo credit in the description. By explaining that you took the photo, you make it clear who owns the image and that you didn't violate anyone's copyrights.

Be careful to avoid taking photos of copyrighted material, such as an entire article or spread in a magazine or anything that completely reproduces someone else's copyrighted image.

To upload an image as a pin, follow these steps:

1. **Use your browser to navigate to** `http://pinterest.com` **and log in.**

2. **Click the Add + button in the top-right corner of the screen.**

   The Add dialog box appears.

3. **Click the Upload a Pin button.**

   The Upload a Pin dialog box appears.

4. **Click the Browse button to find the image on your computer's hard drive.**

   The File Upload dialog box appears, as shown in Figure 3-7.

Figure 3-7: Upload an image to pin.

5. **Select the image to upload and click Open.**

6. **The Upload a Pin dialog box expands to show the image as well as a drop-down list and a description text box. (See Figure 3-8.)**

7. **Use the drop-down list to select a board.**

8. **Type a description of your pin in the text box.**

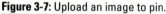

Figure 3-8: Pin an image you uploaded.

9. **Click the Pin It button.**

You're taken directly to the pin's page. Although you can upload images, you can't directly upload video.

Creating a new board on the fly

If you see something you want to pin but don't already have a board that it fits, you don't need to stop in your tracks. You can create a board mid-pin.

Pin as you normally would, but instead of selecting an existing board from the drop-down list, scroll down past all of your boards. You see an option for creating a new board, as shown in Figure 3-9.

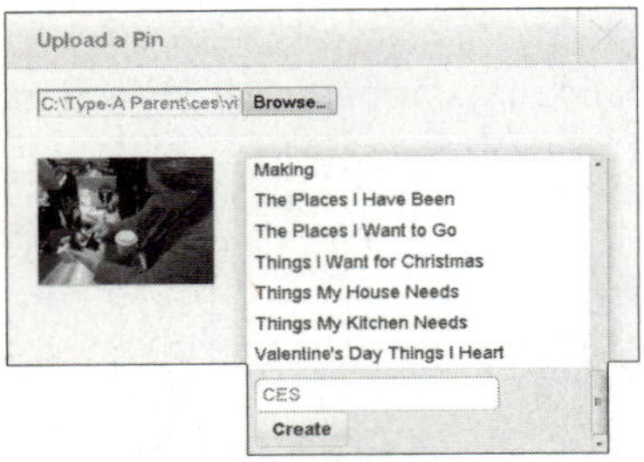

Upload a Pin

C:\Type-A Parent\ces\vi   Browse...

Making
The Places I Have Been
The Places I Want to Go
Things I Want for Christmas
Things My House Needs
Things My Kitchen Needs
Valentine's Day Things I Heart

CES

Create

Figure 3-9: Create a new board as you pin.

Type the name of the new board and click the Create button. Then click the Pin It button, and you have a new pin and a new board.

When you create a board on the fly, it has only a board name. You should later edit the board to add a category and description. (See Chapter 2 to find out how.)

Repinning

When you share another user's existing pin, placing that user's pin on one of your own boards, that's called *repinning*. Repinning is fun and easy, and it's a wonderful way to build up quality pins on your boards quickly. Using repins also allows you to remain active without dedicating massive blocks of time to hunting down great images from around the web to pin. Although you still want to do that as well, I would estimate a large portion of pins on Pinterest are actually repinned.

The upside of Pinterest currently being in invitation-only mode is that the quality of pins is very high, making it a great source for repins. If blatant spam is happening anywhere on Pinterest, I have yet to witness it. In a few minutes of browsing, I can usually find several pins I'm eager to repin. I discuss finding pins worthy of repining in the upcoming sections, but first you need to know how to actually repin a pin.

To repin a pin, follow these steps:

1. **Find a pin that you would like to repin and mouse over it.**

   Three buttons appear: Repin, Like, and Comment. See Figure 3-10.

Repin, Like, and Comment buttons

Figure 3-10: Buttons appear over a pin as you mouse over it.

2. **Click the Repin button.**

   The Repin dialog box appears.

3. **Use the drop-down list to choose which of your boards to use for the repin.**

   If needed, you can also use this drop-down list to create a new board, as described in the earlier section, "Creating a new board on the fly."

4. **Type a description of the pin in the text box.**

   Often you can use the existing description, but sometimes you might need to change the description to your own words. See the later section, "Changing or crediting the original pinner's comments," for more details.

5. **Click the Pin It button.**

   A box flashes with the option to view the pin now. If you don't click it, you're taken back to the page where you repinned.

Finding pins to repin

You can find pins to repin in several ways. Your repins can come both from those Pinterest members you follow and from the general Pinterest membership. Use the following sections as your guide while hunting for great pins on the Pinterest site.

Browsing the stream of people you follow

A great place to start is by looking at the pins in the stream of people you follow. When you signed up, Pinterest automatically set you up to follow some people with similar interests and possibly your Facebook friends. (See Chapter 1 for more about the sign-up process.)

To see the stream of people you're following, use your browser to navigate to `http://pinterest.com` while logged into Pinterest. The main page is filled with the latest pins from the people you follow, as shown in Figure 3-11.

Figure 3-11: The Pinterest home page shows recent pins of the people you follow.

As you scroll down the main page, it continues to load more of the latest pins.

Browsing categories

Pinterest also has an assortment of categories, which I often use when I want to go outside my own stream. Searching by category can also be great when you're seeking pins for a specific board. The categories range from cars and motorcycles to home décor, and from geeky items to weddings and events.

To browse the latest pins in a category, mouse over (but don't click!) the Everything link in the top-middle of the screen (see Figure 3-12) and click a category from the options.

Mouse over this link to view categories

Figure 3-12: The Pinterest category menu.

After you click a category, the category page functions in the same way as your home page stream of people you follow. Simply mouse over the pin to access the Repin button.

Browsing videos

Much of the emphasis on Pinterest is on pictures and graphics, but you can also pin (and, thus, repin) videos. You can find videos to repin by clicking the Videos link in the top-middle of the screen (see Figure 3-13), and then you can mouse over a video to access the Repin button.

Click this link

Figure 3-13: The Pinterest video page.

The downside to the video page is that, at the time of this writing, there's no way to navigate around videos specifically. For example, you can view all videos from throughout Pinterest, but you can't narrow it down to video pins from the people you follow. You also can't narrow it down to a specific category.

You can use the Pinterest Search box to search for videos on a subject. For example, type **craft videos** into the Search text box in the top-left corner of the page and click the Search button (it looks like a magnifying glass). The results may not be exactly what you're looking for, but at least they'll be narrowed down. This isn't an ideal solution, however, because the results return only videos where your search terms are in the pin's description text.

Using the Pinterest Search feature

Pinterest has a Search feature for finding pins, boards, and users. The Search text box is located in the top-left corner of any page on the site. (See Figure 3-14.) You can type a search term in the Search text box and then click the Search button (the magnifying glass icon) to perform a search.

Search box

Search button

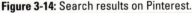

Figure 3-14: Search results on Pinterest.

After you've clicked the Search button, you see results. The default results are pins that match your terms. You can then filter your search results by boards or people by clicking your choice (a text link for Boards or People) just above the results.

The Pinterest Search feature isn't always reliable and sometimes returns an error. It also doesn't seem to pull all pins into results. (Recent pins in testing don't appear at the top of the search result page, for example.) If you're having trouble finding something on Pinterest, you can alternatively search for it on Google; type **site:pinterest.com** followed by your search term in the Google search bar. For example, to search for *Star Wars* pins or boards, type **site:pinterest.com Star Wars** into the Google search box.

You can also use the top menu to find pins by category as an alternative to search, as well as products that have been pinned. To do so, mouse over Everything and then click a category to see results.

Locating a specific user's pins

To find a specific user's pins, conduct a search for the user's name or username and then click the People link below the Search text box. The search results page changes to show profiles with the search term instead of pins.

If the person you're searching for is also a friend you follow or who follows you, you can click your name in the top-right corner of the Pinterest home page to get to your profile page. From there, directly under your name at the top left of the screen, click where it lists a number, followed by followers or following (for example, 100 followers or 100 following) to get a list of people you follow (following) or, who follow you (followers).

Finding pins from a specific website

Although this trick isn't obvious, you can search for existing pins that have come from a specific website as well. The easiest way to do this is to enter the website's main domain in your browser's address bar in the format pinterest.com/source/*DOMAIN.COM*, replacing *DOMAIN.COM* with the site you're interested in. Figure 3-15 shows pins from Wiley.com.

Figure 3-15: A page of pins from a specific website.

Here's another handy trick: If you see a pin and want to find other content from the source where the pin came from, you can do just that. From any pin's page or the lightbox pop-up for a specific pin, you can see a list of other pins from that site; at the bottom right below the pin's image you will see Pinned via [method] from [source]. (See Figure 3-16.) Clicking the source domain will take you to a list of other pins from that site.

Click this link

Figure 3-16: You can find the source of a pin.

Changing or crediting the original pinner's comment

When you repin, Pinterest automatically populates the repin's description with the original pinner's comment. Many times, this isn't an issue, and you can leave it as is.

Sometimes, however, people personalize these descriptions with comments that wouldn't make sense displayed on your board, such as identifying a friend by name who would love it. In other instances, people might be violating the content creator's copyrights by copying and pasting an entire post. (See more on this issue in Chapter 8.) In those cases, you'll want (and need) to change the description.

Adding a few of your own words can make it easy to see repins of your repin in the Pinterest stream. In most cases, people repin without changing the description, and you can recognize those repins when you see your own comments showing up again and again.

You have a few options with descriptions when it comes to repinning:

- ✔ **You can leave the description as is.** This is perfectly appropriate when the description is basic and generic and clearly describes the content pinned.

- ✔ **You can completely change the description by deleting the original pinner's comment and typing in your own.**

- ✔ **You can leave in the original description but place your own comment at the beginning, giving credit to the original pinner. (See Figure 3-17.)** This is typically done by inserting your comment followed by // before the original pinner's comment. Another common method is inserting your own comment at the beginning, followed by "from original pinner:" before the comment.

Figure 3-17: You can add your own description to an original pinner's comment.

Sharing a Pin or Repin on Facebook and Twitter

To share a pin on Twitter or Facebook, you must have the social network integrated into your Pinterest account (as described in Chapter 1). After they're integrated, it's easy to share a repin or a pin on those sites.

As you pin or repin, you'll see the option to check the boxes for Twitter and Facebook. (See Figure 3-18.) When you do, that pin will be posted (on Twitter as a tweet with a link to the pin; on Facebook as an update with a thumbnail of the image and a link to the pin).

You can also share your pins in the same manner — by selecting the check box for Facebook and/or Twitter — when the pin description box pops up.

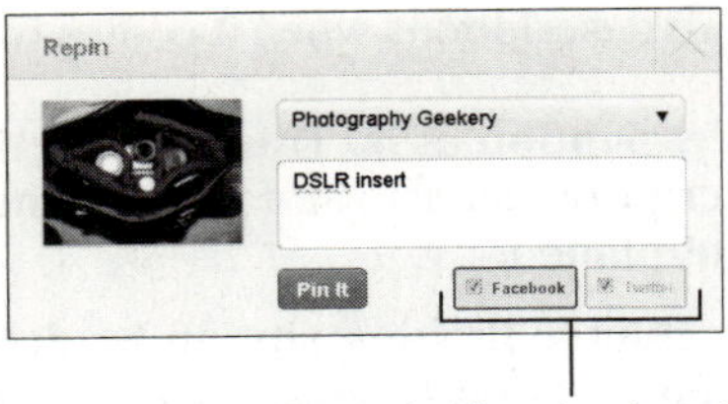

Repin

Photography Geekery ▼

DSLR insert

Pin It | ☑ Facebook | ☑ Twitter

Boxes for Facebook and Twitter

Figure 3-18: You can share on Twitter and Facebook as you repin.

You can get some benefits out of tweeting and Facebook sharing your pins. Sharing helps spread the word that you're on Pinterest and attract followers from your other social networks. It also encourages people on those networks to repin your pins.

It can be easy to pin or repin several things in a very short period of time. You might want to limit which pins you share on Facebook and Twitter so you don't annoy your followers on those networks.

Pinterest offers other options for sharing your pins. See Chapter 4 for more on the ways you can share your pins.

Chapter 4

Socializing on Pinterest

- -

In This Chapter

▶ Locating friends on Pinterest

▶ Following profiles and boards

▶ Gaining followers by sharing your profile link

▶ Sharing pins

- -

To truly experience Pinterest and prosper there, you need to socialize. The core of socializing is finding and interacting with friends and followers, as well as inviting your own friends who are interested in joining Pinterest but haven't yet received the coveted Pinterest invitation.

Finding People to Follow on Pinterest

Chances are good that you already have many friends who are also on Pinterest. Chances are also good that you're going to want to follow some of these individuals. Following a Pinterest member is easy — it's just a matter of finding those people that you want to follow. And in many cases, following a Pinterest member will result in that person following you in return.

On Pinterest, you have *followers* (people who follow your profile) and those you follow, listed under following on your profile. Also, people can follow your boards (some or all) and vice versa.

To find people who are following you so you can follow them back, use these instructions:

1. **Log in to your Pinterest account and click your name in the top-right corner of the screen.**

   Your personal Pinterest page appears.

2. **In the top-right corner of the screen, click the link that states a number followed by the word *followers*.**

   The Your Followers page appears and lists all the people who are currently following all of your boards.

3. **Scroll on the page and click the Follow button next to anyone you want to follow.**

   When you do so, you will be following all of their boards.

To follow any Pinterest member from his or her profile, click the Follow All button in the center of the profile page. When you follow all, you're listed on the user's followers page and included in his count for followers. If you follow only certain boards instead of the Follow All option, however, you aren't listed on the followers page or counted in his follower numbers.

Following Facebook friends on Pinterest

If you have Facebook connected to your Pinterest account, you can quickly find any of your Facebook friends who are also members of Pinterest. To find and follow Facebook friends on Pinterest, follow these steps:

1. **Log in to your Pinterest account, and from the Pinterest home page, mouse over your name in the top-right corner of the screen.**

   A drop-down menu appears.

2. **Choose Find Friends from the drop-down menu.**

   Your Facebook friends who are already Pinterest members are listed in the column on the right, and Facebook friends who aren't on Pinterest yet are listed in the column on the left. (See Figure 4-1.) Although Twitter can be integrated into Pinterest, it doesn't provide the same option for finding Twitter friends who are members of Pinterest.

If your Pinterest account isn't connected to Facebook, instead of a list of friends, you get a big, bold Find Friends from Facebook button. Pinterest doesn't want you to be lonely, so it gives you the option of making the connection. If you click the button, the connection happens instantly if you're logged on to Facebook, and you see the list of your friends.

Facebook friends already on Pinterest

Facebook friends not on Pinterest | Follow All button

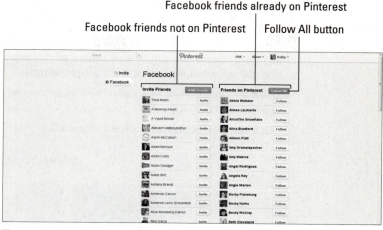

Figure 4-1: You can follow Facebook friends.

3. **Click the Follow All button (refer to Figure 4-1) to quickly follow all of your Facebook friends who are already Pinterest members.**

   Alternatively, you can individually click the Follow button next to a specific name to follow that Facebook friend on Pinterest.

Following individual boards

You can follow a profile (which will put all of the person's pins from all of the person's boards into your homepage stream) or you can pick and choose specific boards to follow. Following specific boards is a great way to focus on content that interests you most.

If you follow a member's specific boards instead of following the member's profile, you aren't included in the member's follower count or appear on his or her list of followers. Pinterest might change this at some point, but for now, that's still a consideration because people can look at a friend's list of followers to find new people to follow. If your goal is to socialize and, in particular, gain more friends, I recommend instead using the Follow All button option with the instructions earlier in this chapter whenever possible.

You can follow a board in a few different ways, and you'll encounter each of these methods as you use and browse Pinterest. You can:

✔ Follow a board from a pin page

✔ Follow a board from a member's profile page

Both of these ways for following a board are simple, two-step processes. To follow a board from a pin page, take these steps:

1. **On a pin page, which is reached by clicking the image of any pin, locate the name and image of the board in which the pin appears and click the Follow button.**

   You can find the board's name and more recent pins to it below the pin image.

2. **Click the Follow button. (See Figure 4-2.)**

Click this button

Figure 4-2: Follow a board from a pin.

To follow a board from a member's profile, take these steps:

1. **Visit the member's profile by clicking his or her name under the pin you like.**

   The member's profile page appears and displays all of the member's boards.

2. **For any board you want to follow, click the Follow button underneath the board name and the thumbnail images of its recent pins. (See Figure 4-3.)**

Click the Follow button to follow that board

Figure 4-3: Follow a board from a member's profile.

TIP

There may come a time when you want to unfollow a board in your stream — perhaps someone is making really annoying pins to a board and you no longer want to follow it. If that's the case, here's how you can unfollow a board:

1. **Click the board name to visit the board. (See Figure 4-4.)**

   As you view the pins in your stream, notice that beneath each pin is the name of the pinner followed by the word *onto*. The text after *onto* is the board name for the board the pin appears on.

Board names appear after the word "onto"

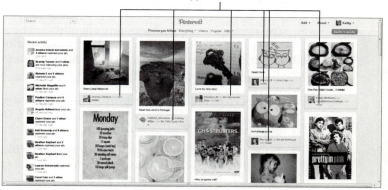

Figure 4-4: The name of a board is linkable on a pin in your stream.

2. **On the board page that appears, click the Unfollow button in the top-center area of the page. (See Figure 4-5.)**

Click this button

Figure 4-5: Opting to unfollow a board.

Adding friends from pins and boards

Another way to find people to follow is to look for pins and boards that interest you and follow the creators. Although you won't know these people personally or have necessarily interacted with them on other social networks, it's a great way to bring pins on the topics you love onto your home page stream.

To find like-minded Pinterest members via pins and boards, you can browse categories or use the Pinterest Search feature. (See Chapter 3 for additional coverage on browsing by categories and using the Pinterest Search feature.)

To find members to follow by category, follow these steps:

1. **Sign in to your Pinterest account.**

2. **From the home page, mouse over the Everything link in the top-middle area of the page and choose a category from the drop-down menu.**

   A new page appears, showing the most recent pins in that category. Because these results are drawn from all users, it's unlikely you'll see someone you're already following. As you browse the pins, you'll see the member's name directly under each pin image. (See Figure 4-6.)

Member names appear under each pin image

Figure 4-6: You can browse users by pin categories.

3. **When you find a pin you like, click the member's name to go to his or her profile page and see all the boards associated with that person.**

4. **Click the Follow All button on the left if you want to follow the user, or click the Follow button under specific boards you want to follow.**

To browse through members to potentially follow via pin search, take these steps:

1. **Conduct a search for a keyword that interests you.**

   See Chapter 3 for information about how the Pinterest Search feature works.

2. **To follow a person who has pins in those results, click his or her name, which appears below the pin image, as shown in Figure 4-7.**

   That user's main Pinterest page appears, showing all the boards the user curates.

3. **Click the Follow All button on the left to follow the user, or click the Follow button under specific boards you want to follow.**

Click a member's name to view their Pinterest page

Figure 4-7: You can browse through members by doing a pin search.

To find members or boards to follow via board search, follow these steps:

1. **Enter a search term that interests you in the Search text box in the top-left corner of the screen.**

   See Chapter 3 for more about how the Pinterest Search feature works.

2. **Click the Boards text link in the top-left corner of the page to filter the results to board names.**

3. **In the results displayed, follow a board by clicking the Follow button under its thumbnail pictures, as shown in Figure 4-8.**

Follow a board by clicking its Follow button

Figure 4-8: You can browse members through a board search.

4. **To follow the person who created the board, click the thumbnail image area to go to that board.**

5. **On the resulting page, click the member's name to the left of the Follow button.**

Do not click the Follow button on this page — that will set you up to follow only the board.

6. **On the profile page, click the Follow All button on the left.**

Don't rely on just one method to find friends. Instead, use a mix of the preceding suggestions to find a diverse mix of people to follow, which in turn creates a diverse mix of pins in your stream.

Inviting friends

When you're on Pinterest, it can be helpful to invite friends to join you there. You might even find that people are in search of an invitation.

To invite a friend, use the following steps:

1. **Log in to Pinterest and click the large, red Invite Friends button in the top-right corner of the home page.**

   The Invite Your Friends to Pinterest page appears, as shown in Figure 4-9.

2. **Enter the e-mail addresses for anyone you want to invite and add a personal note if you like.**

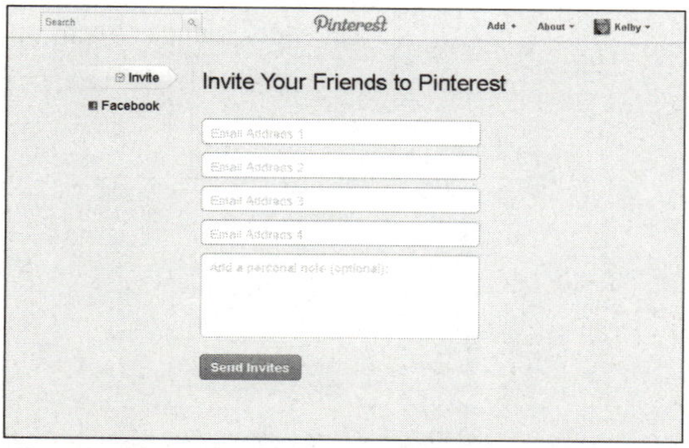

Figure 4-9: Invite friends by their e-mail addresses.

You can also post updates on Twitter on Facebook asking whether people you follow there would like an invitation to Pinterest. Just be sure to ask them to privately send you a message with their e-mail address so you can send the invitation.

You can also invite Facebook friends one by one or all at once. To do so, follow these steps:

1. **Log in to Pinterest and click the large, red Invite Friends button in the top-right corner of the home page.**

   The Invite Your Friends to Pinterest page appears.

2. **Click the Facebook button on the left. (Refer to Figure 4-9.)**

   A screen appears displaying two columns. The column on the left shows Facebook friends who aren't using Pinterest yet and could use an invite; the column on the right shows your Facebook friends who already have Pinterest accounts. (See Figure 4-10.) If you haven't integrated Facebook, you see a Find Friends from Facebook button. If you click that, you can integrate your Facebook account to invite Facebook friends.

3. **To invite everyone at once, click the Invite Friends button at the top of the left column.**

   Alternatively, you can invite friends one at a time by clicking Invite next to each friend's name in the left column.

   Some of your friends might get annoyed if you send bulk invitations to every Facebook friend. I recommend instead inviting Facebook friends one at a time so that you can choose those you think would be most interested in an invitation.

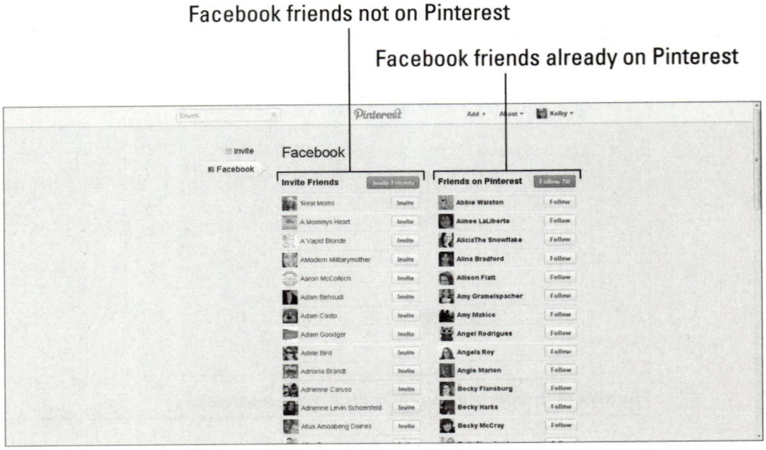

Facebook friends not on Pinterest

Facebook friends already on Pinterest

Figure 4-10: Invite Facebook friends to Pinterest.

Sharing Your Profile Link

If you want to share your Pinterest profile with others so they can follow you or your boards, you need to know and provide the direct link to your profile. Once you know and have the direct link to your profile you can e-mail it to friends, link to it on your blog or website, and share the direct link on social networks.

To find the direct link to your profile, follow these steps:

1. **Log in to Pinterest and click your name in the top-right corner of the screen.**

   The main page for your personal profile appears and displays all the boards you've created.

2. **Make note (either by copying it or writing it down) of the URL in your browser's address bar.**

   The direct link to your profile should be in this format: `http://pinterest.com/YOURUSERNAME/`. (See Figure 4-11.)

Direct link to your profile

Figure 4-11: Find the URL for your profile.

Pinterest also features code you can copy and paste into your website or blog to display either a Follow Me on Pinterest button or a Pinterest icon to invite people to follow your profile. To find this code, perform the following steps:

1. **From the Pinterest home page, mouse over the About button in the top-right corner and choose Pin It Button from the drop-down menu.**

2. **Scroll down the page until you see the section called "Follow Button" for Websites.**

3. **Click whichever button or icon you would like to use. (See Figure 4-12.)**

   After you click a button or icon, the code for it appears to the right of it.

If your readers aren't particularly social media savvy, consider choosing the Follow Me on Pinterest options over the simple P square icon because it's more easily recognized and identified.

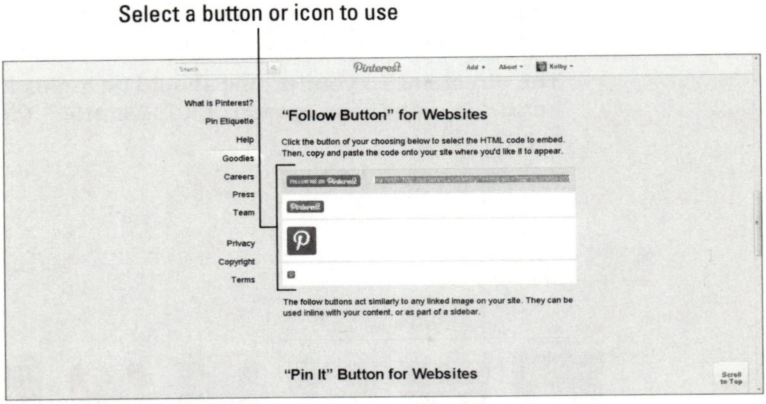

Select a button or icon to use

Figure 4-12: Select a follow button or icon to install on your site.

4. **Highlight and copy the code.**

5. **Paste the code into your site and save.**

You should paste this into your sidebar, not into a specific blog post or page. This might require you get assistance from a webmaster or tech-savvy friend who's familiar with HTML code.

Sharing Pins

Pinterest hosts some great content, which is a primary reason for its surge in usage. Sometimes, you want to do more than repin a pin. You might want to tell a friend about a project that he would love to do for his home, or you could find something so amazing you want to spread the word elsewhere online.

Pinterest provides three key methods for sharing pins outside of Pinterest:

- ✔ E-mailing a pin
- ✔ Sharing a pin on Twitter and Facebook
- ✔ Sharing the direct link to a pin on a blog or website
- ✔ Embedding a pin on a blog or website

Sending pins through e-mail

You can share a pin via e-mail directly from a pin's page. To do that, find a pin you want to share and click it to bring up the pin's individual page. From there, follow these instructions:

1. **To the right of the pin, click the @ Email button, as shown in Figure 4-13.**

    The Email This Pin window appears.

2. **Complete the fields for the recipient's name, e-mail address, and any message you would like to add, as shown in Figure 4-14.**

3. **Click the Send Email button.**

Click this button

Figure 4-13: Find the @ Email button on a pin.

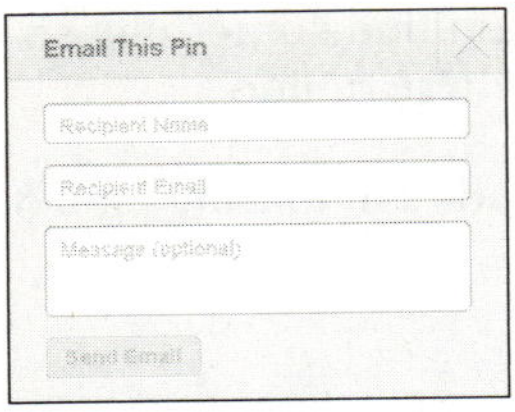

Email This Pin

Recipient Name

Recipient Email

Message (optional)

Send Email

Figure 4-14: The form to send a pin via e-mail.

You can e-mail pins to yourself. I do this regularly when I want to remember a pin beyond adding it to my boards. If you're a frequent pinner, you may have trouble locating the pin later or you might want to add notes to yourself that you don't want to share. You can also e-mail pins to yourself when there's a pin you want to make note of personally but don't want to publicly repin or like.

Sharing pins on Twitter and Facebook

You can either share a pin as you post it yourself or share an existing pin from its page. Sharing pins can be a great way to increase your Pinterest followers as your followers on Twitter and Facebook discover you're also on Pinterest.

To share a pin on Twitter and/or Facebook as you pin or repin, follow these steps:

1. **Create a pin or repin as you normally would.**

   See Chapter 3 for more on pinning and repinning.

2. **When you see the pop-up box to enter the category and description of the pin, select the Twitter check box. (See Figure 4-15.)**

   This box only appears for Twitter if you've integrated it with your Pinterest account. (See Chapter 1 for information on integrating your Pinterest account with social networks.)

3. **Pin or repin the image.**

   After the image is pinned or repined, you see a tweet in your Twitter stream with the description of your pin and a link to the pin page; on Facebook, you see a thumbnail of the pin image with the board name and your description. (See Figure 4-16.)

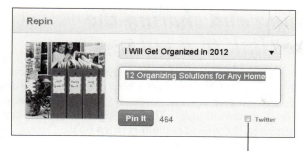

Select Twitter here

Figure 4-15: Set a pin to post on Twitter.

Pinterest pin shared on Facebook

Figure 4-16: A pin on your Facebook wall.

You can also share a pin on Twitter or Facebook from the pin's page. Here are the instructions:

1. **Click the image of a pin to view its detail page.**

   To the right of the pin, you see a Like and a Tweet button (if you've integrated Facebook and Twitter).

2. **Click the Like button to share it on Facebook.**

   Facebook automatically completes the share as soon as you click the button.

3. **Click the Tweet button to share on Twitter.**

   A dialog box appears with a tweet already composed that you can edit as needed.

4. **Click the Tweet button in the box.**

Finding and sharing the direct link to a pin

There are a few reasons you might want the direct link to a pin. Perhaps you want to link to it on a blog, website, or a social network besides Twitter and Facebook. If you're mentioning a specific pin online, you should link to the pin page instead of your main profile (or even the board the pin resides on).

If you're specifically referring to a pin, it's helpful if you direct people to its permalink so they don't have to hunt for it.

Although you can also embed a pin (see the following section), many times a simple link to a pin is preferable or the only option. You can't embed on a social network, for example, and you might not want to take up the real estate on a post or a web page to embed the entire pin.

Embedding pulls in the images as well as the description and source, whereas a direct link can be as simple as a few words that link people to the pin for more information.

To find the pin page URL of one of your own pins, follow these steps:

1. **Visit your Pinterest profile page by clicking your name in the top-right corner.**

2. **Click the image thumbnails for the board that contains the pin.**

   A list of that board's pins appears.

3. **Click the image of the pin you want a link to.**

   That pin's individual page appears.

4. **Copy the URL from your browser's address bar. (See Figure 4-17.)**

5. **When you have the URL, paste it wherever you want to share the link to the pin.**

To link to someone else's pin, you can either find the pin page from your home page, a category page, or a board. In any of those instances, click the image of the pin to go to the pin page and get the URL.

Copy this URL

Figure 4-17: A pin page URL.

Embedding a pin

In some instances, you might want to embed a pin on your own website or blog. For example, if you do a project that's inspired by a pin, you might want to share that pin as well as details of your own experience doing the project.

Just because an image is pinned doesn't necessarily mean the pin was created properly, linking to the original source of the image. Avoid embedding pins that are unlikely to connect to the original source, such as pins of images from Google search, Tumblr, and Yahoo! search.

To embed a pin in your blog or website, follow these steps:

1. **Find the pin you want to share and click it to bring up the pin's individual page.**

2. **Click the <> Embed button to the right of the pin, as shown in Figure 4-18.**

   The Embed Pin on Your Blog window appears and provides the option to set the dimensions of the embedded pin as well as code you can embed on your site. (See Figure 4-19.)

   The image size that's automatically set in the Embed Pin on Your Blog window is the maximum image size to avoid it looking pixelated. You can't make the image bigger, but you can make it smaller.

Click this button

Figure 4-18: Click the Embed button to include a pin on your blog or website.

Figure 4-19: Use the provided Embed code to include a pin on your blog or website.

3. **Copy the embed code.**

4. **Paste the embed code into a location on your blog or site where you can input HTML, such as an HTML or text widget in the sidebar or by clicking the source or code editor in a blog post or page.**

Chapter 5

Using Community Features

*P*interest has a combination of community features you may be familiar with from using sites such as Facebook and Twitter, including liking, commenting, hashtags, and tagging other members.

These community features are more than mere bells and whistles. Hashtags can make it easy to keep track of a Pinterest conversation on one topic, for example, and tagging members can draw a friend's attention to something that interests them.

Interacting with Pins

Although repinning might be the more frequent interaction members have with a pin, you can also comment on a pin or like it. When you comment on a pin, the comment appears below the pin both within your stream and on the pin's individual page. (Figure 5-1 highlights the comments on a pin's page.) If you scroll down on a pin page, you can see who likes the pin, as shown in Figure 5-2.

Liking a pin

Sometimes it makes more sense to like a pin than it does to repin it. You might see a pin that doesn't rise to the level of putting it on your own boards, or maybe you don't have any boards that are a good fit and don't foresee needing such a board. In those cases, you may just want to like the pin rather than repin it.

Comments made about the pin

Figure 5-1: See all the comments on a pin.

Likes for a pin

Figure 5-2: Check out who has liked a pin.

Liking a pin does a couple of things:

✔ It adds to the pin's Like stats and shows that the pin has been endorsed.

✔ It allows you to save the pin for viewing later without having to put it on a board. (I explain how in a minute.)

To like a pin on the Pinterest home page stream, a search page, or a category page, mouse over the image and click the Like button. (See Figure 5-3.)

Click this button

Figure 5-3: Click the Like button on a pin to save it to your profile without pinning it.

To like a pin from its page, click the Like button at the top of the page. The latest pins you've liked appear after you click the Likes tab on your profile page. (See Figure 5-4.)

Commenting on a pin

You can comment on Pinterest pins, which can be a way to add your thoughts, ask questions, and interact with other members. You can comment on a pin directly from the home page stream, a category page, or a search results page.

Pins recently liked are listed here

Figure 5-4: Likes are listed in the recent activity section on your profile page.

To comment on a pin, follow these steps:

1. **Mouse over the pin's image.**

2. **Click the Comment button that appears above the pin's image.**

3. **A text box appears below the pin's image. (See Figure 5-5.)**

4. **Type your comment and then click the Comment button beneath the text box, as shown in Figure 5-5.**

When you comment on a pin, that comment is public. The member whose pin you commented on may receive an e-mail notification, depending on that person's settings. Pinterest does not, however, notify you if someone replies to your comment unless you have asked it to in your e-mail preferences (see Chapter 1). Because there's also no way to see your comment history beyond your most recent activity on your profile page, you may also want to like or repin when you comment so you can revisit the pin later for responses.

Enter your comment here...

then click this button

Figure 5-5: Comment on a pin.

To comment on a pin from a pin page, scroll to the bottom, click where it says Add a Comment (see Figure 5-6), and type your comment. Then click the Post Comment button.

Enter your comment here

Figure 5-6: Add a comment on a pin page.

Customizing and Tagging Pins

There are some tricks that can enhance your pins or add to their functionality. You can use hashtags similar to those found on Twitter, you can tag members' names in pin descriptions, and you can add a price tag ribbon that will appear in the top-left corner of a pin.

Using hashtags

A *hashtag* is a way of tagging a term so that the term becomes *clickable* (this means that when you see a hashtag, you can click on it). You do this by adding a # at the beginning of a word, such as #pinterest.

Hashtags are popular on Twitter and are also used now on the newer Google+ to help filter social media updates. On Pinterest, you can use a hashtag in a pin description. The main difference between a Pinterest hashtag and a hashtag on another social networking site is that clicking a Pinterest hashtag doesn't give you results that also have that hashtag. What it does is conduct a search for that word after the # symbol.

To view results for the search term when you see it in a pin description, click any word that starts with a #. (See Figure 5-7.) Clicking the hashtag takes you to the search results for that word.

If you use a hashtag, it should be something that people would want to search for or be a popular word or term.

A hashtag in a pin's description

Figure 5-7: Click a hashtag in a pin description to see pins that match that search term.

Tagging member names in pins

In a pin description, you can tag another Pinterest member to draw their attention to the pin. Tagging them also makes their profile name in the pin description link to that person's profile.

One thing I've noticed when tagging members is that quite a few members are missing from the available user names, including people I'm following and who are following me back. This glitch could be fixed in the future, but for now, expect some bugs. In testing, I have found that if both members unfollow and refollow each other's profiles (via Follow All, not following specific boards), the issue is fixed.

To tag a member while pinning, repining, or commenting, follow these steps:

1. **In a pin description or a comment, type the @ character and the first letter(s) of the name of the person you want to tag in the description without a space.**

   Type **@k**, for example, to tag me.

   A drop-down list of friends whose names start with that letter appears, as shown in Figure 5-8.

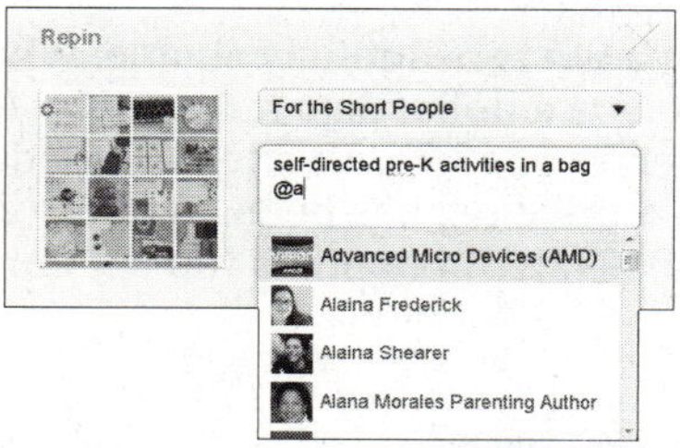

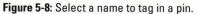

Figure 5-8: Select a name to tag in a pin.

2. **From the drop-down list, select the name of the person you want to tag.**

   The name is filled out in that spot in the description.

3. **Finish writing your comment or description and then click the Comment or Repin button to publish.**

   After you tag the person, the description of the pin features her name, and it will be linked to her profile page. (See Figure 5-9.)

A tagged name

Figure 5-9: A tagged name in a pin description.

Including a price tag in a pin

Including a price tag with a pin is beautifully simple. When writing a description of a pin, include a dollar sign followed by the number of the price, such as either $1 or $3.25. This feature is ideal when pinning a product. When a price tag has been added to a pin, the pin is displayed with a price tag ribbon in its top-left corner. (See Figure 5-10.)

Price tag ribbon

Figure 5-10: A pin with a price tag ribbon.

Any time you include a dollar sign in a pin, it adds a price tag ribbon to the image. Some pins simply refer to a price to do a project where this might not make sense. If you wish to avoid having a price tag on a pin, don't use the $ symbol (for example, say a project cost five dollars to make).

 When you use the price tag feature on a pin, the pin will be pulled into the Gifts section, which you can find from the Pinterest home page. Click the Gifts link in the top-middle area of the Pinterest home page. Under the Gifts menu, pins are organized by price. (See Figure 5-11.)

Click here to view the Gifts section

Figure 5-11: The Gifts page organized by price range.

Chapter 6

Finding Ways to Use Pinterest

- -

In This Chapter

▶ Using Pinterest to plan a project

▶ Gathering pins for weddings and other events

▶ Shopping with Pinterest

▶ Utilizing Pinterest for self-improvement

▶ Using Pinterest as a bookmark site

▶ Making use of Pinterest for business and work

▶ Employing Pinterest to support a cause

- -

*P*interest is fun, but it also has many practical purposes. People are using Pinterest for planning weddings, creating shopping wish lists, renovating their homes, organizing their lives, losing weight, teaching their children, getting dinner inspiration, collaborating with co-workers, and so much more.

 This chapter covers some of the more popular ideas for using Pinterest, but you're not limited to these. If you're putting effort into a project that can involve images or videos, Pinterest can help you.

Planning a Project with Pinterest

One of the most productive ways you can use Pinterest is to plan a project. The pinboard interface makes it easy to put several ideas or references in one location.

Improving, decorating, and organizing your home

You can use Pinterest to plan a home-improvement project, decorate a room, or get rid of all that annoying clutter. Many boards on Pinterest are dedicated to some form of home improvement.

You can create a general board on home improvement (see Figure 6-1), or you can be very precise and create a board for a specific room, project, or topic, such as organization. (See Figure 6-2.) For instance, I have a board dedicated to organizing my kitchen pantry.

Figure 6-1: A general home board.

Figure 6-2: A board on organizing the home.

Some options for pins for boards about the home include the following:

- ✔ Paint color schemes
- ✔ Do-it-yourself (DIY) tutorials
- ✔ Products you need to buy
- ✔ Examples of décor you like
- ✔ Finished project images to help with ideas
- ✔ Articles, blog posts, and websites with tips

Getting craft ideas

Easily one of the most popular uses of Pinterest is for craft ideas, with a tremendous amount of sharing of project DIYs. This is another area where it can be helpful to have a general craft board, as shown in Figure 6-3, or one with a narrow focus on something like knitting, as shown in Figure 6-4. You can also do both. Another option is to have a board for seasonal and holiday-specific crafts. (See Figure 6-5.)

Creating a craft board can be a great way to save inspiration, ideas, and instructions for when you have time to complete the crafts.

 To find pins to include on a craft board, check out the Pinterest category for DIY and Crafts by going to the Pinterest home page, mousing over the Everything link at the top, and choosing that category from the drop-down menu.

Figure 6-3: A general craft board.

Figure 6-4: A narrow-focus craft board.

Figure 6-5: A holiday craft board.

Travel planning

Pinterest can be of great help for planning an upcoming trip (see Figure 6-6) or for sharing the cities you've visited and the ones you'd love to visit one day.

Figure 6-6: A trip-planning board.

For trip planning, you can use Pinterest to help collect and organize ideas for things to do and places to stay as you roam away from home. You can also pin several resources to have on hand during your trip, especially if you've a smartphone and can access your pinboard while you're on your trip. You can even use a smartphone to take photos while traveling to pin to your board. See Chapter 7 for more about going mobile with Pinterest.

Here are just a few ideas for pins on a board for a vacation:

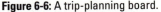 Yelp! results for restaurants, attractions, and hotel. (Yelp! is a website with detailed information and reviews on local dining, hotels, and sights.)

- ✓ Local tourism office sites and resources
- ✓ Official sites for sights, restaurants (perhaps with menus), shops, hotels, and public transportation
- ✓ Images of things to see while visiting
- ✓ Websites, blogs, and newspapers covering the region
- ✓ Maps for the city, region, country, and public transportation
- ✓ Photos that you take during your travels

Cooking

The quantity and quality of recipes on Pinterest is astounding. You can find recipes and tutorials for just about any type of food: everything from gluten-free meals to greasy soul food. You can create a general food board (see Figure 6-7), but if cooking is your passion, you might consider creating multiple food boards for specific types of recipes.

You should never copy the entire content of a page as your pin description. Instead, copy the name of the recipe (for example, "chocolate chip cookie recipe"). The pin should link to the original content with the full recipe and instructions. Copying the entire post is a violation of that writer's copyrights.

Figure 6-7: A general food board.

Some example ideas for food and recipe boards include the following:

- ✓ Boards by meal or course for things like dinner planning, school packed lunches or soup recipes (see Figure 6-8).
- ✓ Boards by ethnic cuisine type
- ✓ Boards by preparation (baking, pastries, canning, or slow cooker, for example)

✔ Boards by season, such as recipes for fixing picnic treats in the summer or for baking fall harvest foods (squash, apples, and so on)

✔ Boards by holiday, such as Christmas recipes

✔ Boards by specific diet type

Figure 6-8: An example of a food board by course.

People see only the image and your description with your pin. Instead of using a description that's general, such as "yummy," be sure to say what exactly is depicted in the photo, such as "Easy Tomato Bisque recipe from AllRecipes.com."

Learning and teaching

Instructors and students alike use Pinterest for a wide variety of educational purposes. You can find boards dedicated to learning activities for toddlers, as well as boards on learning adult skills such as photography and writing. In fact, tutorials on the web are frequently pinned on Pinterest.

Infographics, or a visual representation of statistics, are very popular on Pinterest, so consider using Pinterest as a way to research and pin statistics for future reference. Many people who homeschool are using Pinterest to pin ideas for learning activities, for example. (See Figure 6-9.) Book clubs and websites are using Pinterest to share recommended books.

Pinterest can be a great place to collect teaching tools for children, from printable flash cards and worksheet pages to tutorials on science and art projects. You can create a general board for ideas for teaching children or create boards that are age- or grade-specific, subject-specific, and so on.

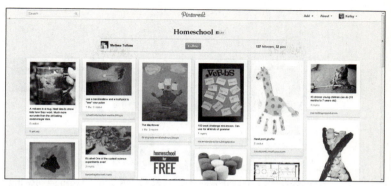

Figure 6-9: A homeschool board at `http://pinterest.com/ matulloss/homeschool`.

Pinterest is also a great place for adult learning. Many boards are related to social media. Photography is a popular topic. (See Figure 6-10.) Boards on crafts, knitting, and other hobbies are prolific. How-to steps and tutorials are also popular on Pinterest.

Figure 6-10: My photography board at `http://pinterest.com/ kelby/photography-geekery`.

Using Pinterest for Weddings and Other Events

Wedding planning is an ideal (and popular) use for Pinterest. Because planning a wedding tends to be very visual, the site is a natural aid for this purpose. Many boards are dedicated to a couple's ideas for their own wedding (see Figure 6-11), and plenty of boards are dedicated to general wedding inspiration.

Figure 6-11: A board used for ideas for a specific person's wedding.

To find a board in a specific topic, use the Search text box at the top of the site. Just above the results, click Boards to filter only board results. See more tips on searching in Chapter 3.

Pinterest is also a great way to share images of events such as festivals, conferences (see Figure 6-12), and performances. Beyond sharing on Pinterest, you can also follow events at home by finding related boards.

Figure 6-12: USA Today created a board for its coverage of Consumer Electronics Show (CES).

Creating a group board for an event

A group board can enable people to share ideas for planning an event or to share content pre-event. You could use a group board during an event to allow many people to share live images and content. A group board can even be used post-event to share. In fact, you can use it for all three!

Here are a few ideas for group board pin content:

- ✔ Add members of the wedding party and family to help share ideas for a wedding.

- ✔ Add guests of a wedding and let them post pictures of the couple or of graphics with well wishes for the couple.

- ✔ Create a conference or an event board and add attendees so they can share topical content and/or their own sites.

- ✔ Create an event board for organizers and staff to share ideas to help with planning the event.

To create a group pinboard, follow these steps:

1. **Log in to your Pinterest account.**

2. **Click the Add+ button in the top-right corner of the screen.**

   The Add dialog box appears.

3. **Click the Create a Board option (see Figure 6-13).**

   The Create a Board dialog box appears.

Click this option

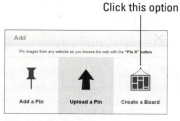

Figure 6-13: Add a board.

4. **Type the board name and select a category (such as Weddings and Events).**

5. **Select the radio button for Me + Contributors next to the Who Can Pin? question.**

6. **Type the first letter(s) of a person's name in the text box.**

   Pinterest displays a list of members that match. (See Figure 6-14.) The tricky part here is it sometimes goes alphabetically by username and sometimes by real name, but the list displays the user's real name.

7. **Click the name you want to add and then click the Add button.**

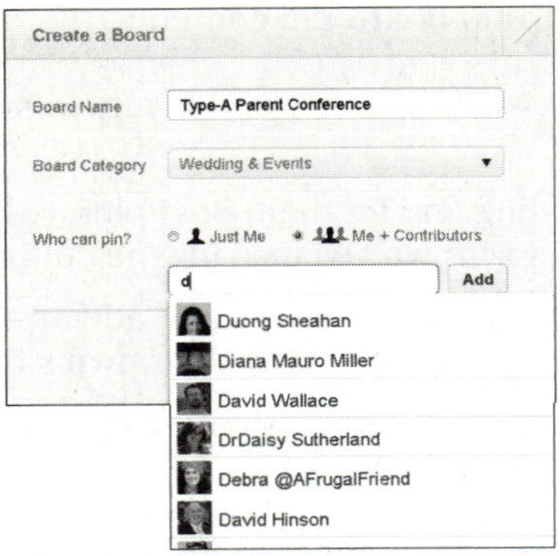

Figure 6-14: Finding names of members to add to a group board.

8. **Repeat Steps 6 and 7 until you've added everyone.**

   You can also add just a few people up front and then edit the board after it's created (see Chapter 2 to find out more about editing boards) to add more people, as shown in Figure 6-15.

 To add people to a board, you must be following their Pinterest profile (not just certain boards of theirs), and they must be following your Pinterest profile (not just some of your boards). People are only considered a follower when they follow all of a person's boards.

 Many people have reported that creating group boards on Pinterest is glitchy. For example, sometimes you can't add someone to your group board even though you're both following each other's Pinterest profile. If you find you can't add someone to a board, you may be able to correct the issue by unfollowing the person and then re-following him and asking him to also unfollow and re-follow you.

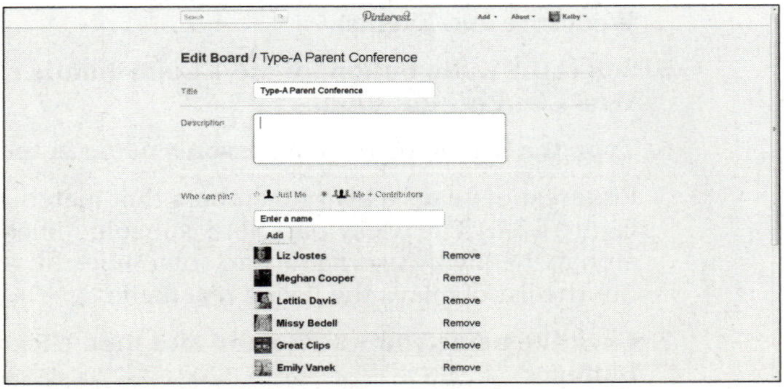

Figure 6-15: Editing a board to add new members.

Creating a hashtag for an event

For sharing information on Pinterest about an event, consider using a unique hashtag (see Chapter 5 for more on hashtags) and sharing it with others attending the event. Doing so makes it easy for anyone to follow along.

Avoid common phrases and instead create a hashtag that's unlikely to be used for content and pins outside of the event. If it's a common phrase, it can be confusing because hashtags do a general search for those terms.

To create a hashtag, you need to add the coding for a hashtag in a pin's description. You create hashtags by placing a # character before a term; the format for coding a hashtag is #term. (See Figure 6-16.) The term you use should be one word, no spaces, and no special characters. If you will use more than one word in a hashtag, you should leave no space between. For example, a two-word hashtag would be #twowords.

A hashtag in a pin's description

Figure 6-16: Use of a clickable hashtag in a pin description.

To search the hashtag, click it in a description. (Pinterest automatically converts into a search link.)

To encourage others to search for pins in the hashtag, share the URL you find in your browser's address bar after you click the linkable hashtag. The URL will be in the format `pinterest.com/search/?q=TERM`.

Utilizing Pinterest for Shopping

Pinterest is a natural for shopping. First, it's visual much like an online shopping site. Second, Pinterest allows you to label pins with prices by adding price tags to them. (See Chapter 5 to find out more about price tags.) Pinterest also includes a Gift link in the top-middle area of the Pinterest home page (see Figure 6-17); click the Gift link and use the drop-down menu to sort and view pins by price.

The Gifts link

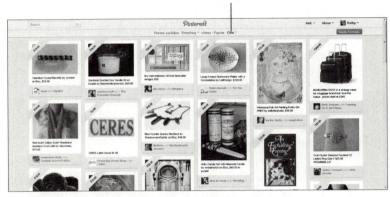

Figure 6-17: The main Gifts page with pins that have price tags.

You can also use Pinterest to research products before you buy them. For example, if you're buying a car or a major appliance, create a board with different models you're considering, reviews of the different models, various retailers that sell the product, how much the retailers sell it for, and so on.

You can also use Pinterest to self-promote and encourage sales of your own products, but you should strictly limit your self-promotion on Pinterest. See more on using Pinterest to self-promote in Chapter 10.

Creating a wish list

Pinterest can be a great site for creating a wish list. Unlike some other popular sites with wish lists tied to their own products, you can pin any product with an image from any site.

You can create wish list boards for specific occasions, such as birthdays, baby showers, a wedding gift registry, and Christmas, or for specific product categories such as jewelry or gadgets. You can also simply create a wish list board and pin anything you would love to receive as a gift. Figure 6-18 shows an example of a wish list.

Figure 6-18: A personal wish list.

 You can use the pin's description to specify details such as the size or color you would prefer.

Finding products

One of the easiest methods for finding products on Pinterest is to use Gift link in the top-middle area of the Pinterest home page. When you mouse over that the Gift link, a drop-down menu appears with different price levels. Select a price level to view the page of pins for items in that price range. (See Figure 6-19.) When you see products you like, repin them to your wish list board.

When you see products on other websites, use the Pin It Button to post the product to your board. (Check out Chapter 3 to find out more.) If you include a price with dollar sign (in the format $1) in your description, Pinterest includes the price as a price tag on the pin itself. (See Chapter 5 to find out more about price tags.)

Finding share-worthy products

It can also be fun to use Pinterest to share products that you may not plan to buy or want as a gift but would just love to share. Unique, beautiful, funky, interesting, and funny products are the ones most likely to get repinned, liked, and commented on.

Select a price range

Figure 6-19: The Gifts drop-down menu of price ranges and the $500 and up Gifts page.

You can also share products you see on a store's shelves by taking a picture from your mobile phone. (See Chapter 7.) That can be a great way to find ideas for your own wish list, in fact. If you do so, however, just be sure you include enough information for someone to know the source of the image (the product name), where to buy it (the store name), and the price.

Using Pinterest for Self-Improvement

Many people use Pinterest for some form of self-improvement, whether it's losing a few pounds or sharing quotes that motivate and inspire.

Dieting and fitness with Pinterest

You can use Pinterest for a wide variety of methods of dieting and losing weight. You can create multiple boards, such as one for healthy recipes, one for strength training instructions, and one for yoga. (See Figure 6-20.) You can also simply create one catch-all board for anything related to weight loss and fitness. I've seen some people who have boards with clothing they hope to fit into one day, and others with boards that are entirely made up of pins of quotes that motivate you to work out.

Figure 6-20: A targeted fitness board on yoga.

You can find content, exercise tutorials, and healthy recipes all over the Internet, and Pinterest is a great source. You can use the Pinterest Search feature (see Chapter 3) to find boards and pins on specific health, diet, and fitness topics. Pinterest also has a Fitness page (see Figure 6-21); simply mouse over the Everything link in the top-middle area of the Pinterest home page and choose Fitness from the drop-down menu that appears.

Figure 6-21: The Pinterest Fitness page.

Finding motivational quotes

When you're active on Pinterest, you quickly notice that images of popular quotes and motivational phrases are abundant. Creating a board for these sayings can be great when you need a pick-me-up, need business and work motivation, want inspiration to be creative, or just could use a good laugh.

The Humor page (which you can find by mousing over the Everything link in the top-middle area of the Pinterest home page and choosing Humor from the drop-down menu) can be a great place to find funny quotes, sayings, comics, and posters. (See Figure 6-22.) You can also do searches (see Chapter 3) for terms such as *quotes* (see Figure 6-23), *inspiration,* and *motivation.*

Figure 6-22: The Pinterest Humor page.

Figure 6-23: A search for the term *quotes.*

Making Use of Pinterest as a Bookmark Site

You certainly have plenty of ways to save your favorite websites: using your browser's bookmarking feature, using other bookmarking sites such as StumbleUpon, sharing on social networks such as Facebook, or using a feed reader.

Pinterest, however, can be a great site for saving the sites, blog posts, and articles for later reading or reference. Because Pinterest is visual, it makes for a pleasant way to scan your bookmarks.

You can create a To Read Later board so you can quickly bookmark an article to save until you have time for it. You can create boards for favorite sites in a certain category, such as Favorite Gift Shops, Favorite Blogs (see Figure 6-24), or Favorite News Sites.

Figure 6-24: A board with favorite blogs and sites.

Employing Pinterest for Business and Work

For your work or business, you can use Pinterest for ideas, project management, and collaboration with staff or co-workers. It can also be useful for promoting your business. (Chapter 10 covers using Pinterest for promotion.)

For example, some boards are dedicated entirely to business card designs, such as the one shown in Figure 6-25. You could create a board for office design or supplies, or for industry-related sites.

Figure 6-25: A business card board.

You can use collaborative boards with employees, co-workers, or clients to share ideas for projects and work.

Using Pinterest to Support a Cause

Spreading the word about a cause can be well suited to Pinterest because it allows others who are passionate about the cause to like, repin, and comment.

You can create a board to pin causes that you're passionate about. (See Figure 6-26.) This can help grow awareness for the cause and can also be used as a reference when you want to donate or volunteer. Some causes on Pinterest even share information, tips, and related content as well. (See Figure 6-27.)

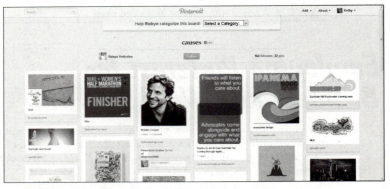

Figure 6-26: A board featuring various causes and charities.

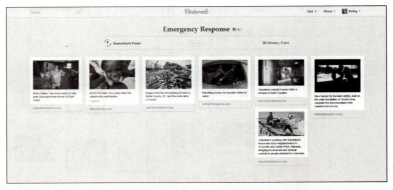

Figure 6-27: The nonprofit Samaritan's Purse has a board highlighting global emergencies.

Chapter 7

Going Mobile with Pinterest

*P*interest is easy to use on a mobile device. In fact, some people use it primarily on a mobile device because it has a simple design that makes it easy to use Pinterest any time.

The mobile version of the Pinterest site (http://m.pinterest.com; see Figure 7-1) can be used on any mobile device that has touchscreen functionality. If your mobile device doesn't have a touchscreen, the mobile site won't work properly.

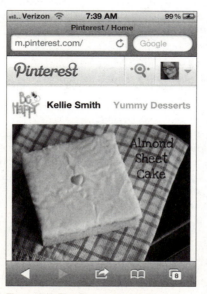

Figure 7-1: The Pinterest mobile site.

Pinterest has also developed a Pinterest app for the iPhone, which is listed as developed by Cold Brew Labs in the iTunes Store. Although third-party apps exist for the iPhone, most currently have bad reviews. Because you can create essentially the same functionality via the official Pinterest app, I don't recommend it at this writing.

The one functionality that you might seek in an iPhone app is the ability to pin easily from the Safari browser. The best-rated third-party app for that option is Pinterest (developed by Ronen Drihem) and costs 99 cents to download.

It's worthwhile to keep an eye on new Pinterest apps as they appear in the iTunes Store. Examine reviews in the iTunes Store (listed at the bottom of an app's information page) to find ones that are well recommended by users.

 If you're new to Pinterest, the Pinterest app can actually be easier and less overwhelming to use than the Pinterest desktop website. Though the Pinterest app has fewer features, it results in a simplified interface.

Users have made many complaints that Pinterest hasn't yet released an app for Android or other smartphones. I expect more apps will be created — both by Pinterest and by third parties — in the coming months due to the popularity of Pinterest.

 Routinely search your mobile device's app store or market for Pinterest apps. Because the site is growing quickly in popularity, apps are likely to be released both for using the site as well as other functionality, such as adding pins from your mobile device's camera or web browser.

Installing the Pinterest App for the iPhone

The Pinterest app for the iPhone makes it easy to view your friends' pins and to repin items when you're out and about (and even when you're relaxing at home). You can also view the latest activity related to your pins (such as comments, likes, and repins of your shared pins), your basic profile, as well as a list of your latest pins and all of your boards.

To install the Pinterest app for the iPhone, follow these steps:

1. **Go to the App Store on your phone.**

2. **Search for the term *Pinterest*.**

   A list of apps relevant to Pinterest appears.

3. **Find the main Pinterest app (developed by Cold Brew Labs) in the list of search results and tap the Install button.**

   The Pinterest app Info page appears.

4. **Tap the Install button in the top-right corner of the screen. (See Figure 7-2.)**

   The Apple ID Password screen appears.

5. **Type in your password and tap OK.**

   The app icon appears on your screen, and a progress bar below it indicates the download progress.

6. **When the app is done downloading, tap the app icon to open it.**

   The login screen appears, as shown in Figure 7-3.

7. **Choose Facebook or Twitter to log in with (be sure to use one you currently have integrated with your Pinterest account; see Chapter 1) and authorize the app through the instructions on either Facebook or Twitter.**

   Alternately, you can log in with your Pinterest account e-mail and password.

8. **Tap the Login button.**

   The Push Notifications window appears. Push notifications will pop up an alert when your Pinterest account has activity.

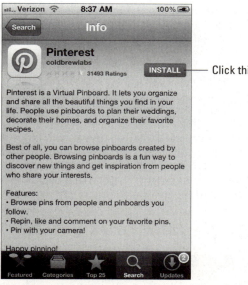

Figure 7-2: Install the Pinterest app.

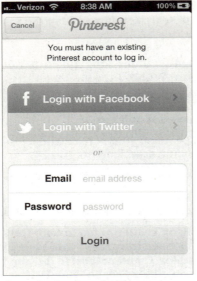

Figure 7-3: Log in to the Pinterest app.

9. **Tap either Don't Allow or Allow, depending on your preference for push notifications.**

   The Pinterest app launches.

After you've installed and launched the Pinterest app, you see the app in its logged-in format, which includes the Pinterest logo at the top of the screen and a menu at the bottom with icons for different tabs in the app. The tab you're currently viewing is indicated by which icon at the bottom is red.

The Pinterest app will revert to full-screen viewing while scrolling pins. To see the menu again, touch and keep your finger on the screen and move your finger down.

You can refresh from several screens in the apps. To refresh the screen, touch and keep your finger on the top of the screen, move your finger down, and then release your finger from the screen. You'll know whether the page you're on is a page that can be refreshed if you do this gesture and receive a message saying Release to Refresh.

Using the Following tab in the iPhone app

The icon on the far left of the menu on the bottom of the screen is the Following tab. This is the default tab that you see when you launch the app. (See Figure 7-4.) The Following tab shows you the latest pins from the people and the boards you follow. You can return to the Following tab at any time by tapping the Following icon.

When you're viewing the Following tab, you can scroll down the screen to see more of the latest pins from people and boards you follow. You can also tap an image to go to the original, off-site source of the pin if it has one. Each pin has a Repin and Like button below the pin's description (refer to Figure 7-4) that you can tap to repin or like it.

To the right of the Repin and Like buttons is a More button. Tap the More button to get a number of additional options, as shown in Figure 7-5.

Figure 7-4: The default Following tab for the Pinterest app.

The More button gives you the following options:

- ✔ **Comment:** Allows you to leave a comment on a pin.
- ✔ **Share on Facebook:** Use this to post the pin as an update to your Facebook wall.
- ✔ **Share on Twitter:** This option allows you to share the link on Twitter.

Figure 7-5: Tap the More button on a pin to get this menu of options.

 ✓ **Save to Camera Roll:** This option puts the image of the pin in your gallery.

   Be aware that it's likely the image is copyrighted by someone else — if it's a copyrighted image, you shouldn't share it outside of Pinterest.

 ✓ **Email Pin:** Sends an e-mail to someone to check out the pin with its direct link.

   If you want to save a pin for future reference but don't want to publicly like or repin it, you can use this option to e-mail it to yourself.

Utilizing the Explore tab in the iPhone app

The second icon from the left in the menu on the bottom of the screen is for the Explore tab. Tap this tab to see a menu of the Pinterest categories. (See Figure 7-6.)

You can use the Search function at the top to find pins, boards, or people related to a specific term, or scroll down to see the full list of categories. Tap a category to see recent pins for that category. (See Figure 7-7.) Tap Explore to return to the list of categories.

Verizon 📶	9:04 AM	100% 🔋

Pinterest

Architecture	>
Art	>
Cars & Motorcycles	>
Design	>
DIY & Crafts	>
Education	>
Film, Music & Books	>
Fitness	>
Food & Drink	>

Following   Explore   📷   Activity   Profile

Figure 7-6: A menu of Pinterest categories under the Explore tab.

Figure 7-7: View pins by category in the app.

From the screen of pins (see Figure 7-7), you can click any pin to see its individual pin page. You find the same options that are available on pins on the Following tab — the Repin, Like, and More buttons.

Pinning your photographs with your iPhone

The camera icon in the middle of the menu on the bottom of the screen is for (you guessed it) your iPhone's camera. Tapping the camera icon allows you to take a photo with your iPhone's camera and upload it directly to Pinterest.

To take and upload a photo to Pinterest, follow these instructions:

1. **Launch the Pinterest app and tap the camera icon.**

   You see the typical iPhone camera shooting screen, as shown in Figure 7-8.

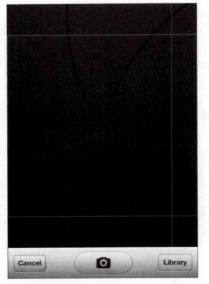

Figure 7-8: Take a photo to upload to Pinterest.

2. **Take a photo as you normally would by tapping the Camera button.**

   After you take the picture, you can move the image around the square capture area by dragging the picture. You can also scale the image by using two fingers to stretch out or pinch in on the screen.

3. **Tap the Use button when you're done moving and scaling the image.** Next, you can touch up the photo's color. Click Use again when it is ready.

4. **At the prompt, choose whether or not to allow Pinterest to share your location.** If you have notifications off and are not prompted, you can turn Place on or off on the next screen.

Keep in mind that if you share your location people will know exactly where you're at when sharing. If you're at home, for example, you may not want to publicize your location.

5. **Complete the pin description and choose a board to pin the image to.**

You can decide here as well whether to include the location by turning the Place option on or off. You can also choose to share on Facebook and Twitter by tapping the toggle from Off to On.

6. **Tap the Pin It button in the top-right corner of the screen.**

You're bounced to the default Following screen with a progress bar at the top of the screen. When the upload is complete, a black box with a `Pinned` message pops up briefly and then disappears.

You can also use any photo in your iPhone image gallery instead. To use a photo in your gallery, follow these steps:

1. **Launch the Pinterest app and tap the camera icon in the middle of the menu on the bottom of the screen.**

2. **Tap the Library button in the bottom-right of the screen. (Refer to Figure 7-8.)**

Your iPhone's Photo app opens.

3. **Within the Photos app, tap Camera Roll (see Figure 7-9) or the photo album that has the photo you want to pin.**

4. **Tap to select the image you want and then move and scale the image. (See Figure 7-10.)**

You can move the image around the square capture area by dragging the picture. You can also scale the image by using two fingers to stretch out or pinch in on the screen.

5. **Tap the Choose button in the bottom-right corner of the screen.**

The Tap and Drag screen appears, as shown in Figure 7-11.

6. **Tap and drag to brighten or darken the image.**

7. **Tap the Use button in the bottom-right corner of the screen.**

The Add a Pin screen appears, as shown in Figure 7-12.

Figure 7-9: Choose a photo album from your iPhone image library.

Figure 7-10: Move and scale an image for a pin.

Figure 7-11: Tap and drag to brighten or darken your image.

8. **Complete the description, choose a board, decide whether to share your location, and choose whether or not to share on Twitter or Facebook.**

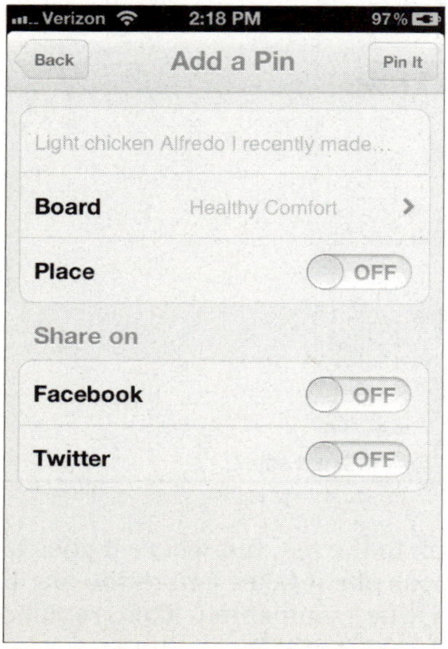

Figure 7-12: Entering the details for your image pin.

9. **Tap the Pin It button in the top-right corner of the screen.**

You're bounced to the default Following screen with a progress bar at the top of the screen. When the upload is complete, a black box with a `Pinned` message pops up briefly and then disappears.

You should share photos directly only if you have the rights to the image and took the photo yourself to avoid copyright infringement. See more on this issue in Chapter 8.

Checking recent Pinterest activity by using your iPhone

The second icon from the right in the menu on the bottom of the screen is the Activity tab. Tapping the Activity tab displays a list of notifications for any recent repins and likes of your pins, comments on your pins, as well as new people following you or your boards. (See Figure 7-13.)

Figure 7-13: The Activity tab in the Pinterest app.

You can tap a notification in the list, but where it goes is limited. If you click the icon of your pin, it takes you to the pin. If you click the name of the member who commented, liked, repinned, or followed you, it takes you to their profile.

Viewing and updating your profile

The icon on the far right of the menu on the bottom of the screen is the Profile tab, and this tab has several options. Using the Profile tab, you can quickly view your number of followers and the number of people you follow, and you can browse your boards, latest pins, and your likes. You can also find instructions for pinning websites directly from the Safari browser.

The Profile tab defaults to your main Profile screen and displays your basic profile information at the top of the screen and your latest pins displayed beneath. (See Figure 7-14.)

Below your profile picture and the number of followers and people you're following are three tabs; from left to right, they're Boards, Pins, and Likes. Your profile defaults to the middle tab, Pins, where you can see thumbnail images of your latest pins.

Tap the Boards tab to see a list of all of your boards, as shown in Figure 7-15.

You can scroll down to see all boards, and you can tap the name of any board to view a screen displaying the thumbnails of your most recent pins to that board. From there, you can tap a pin's image and see the pin's page and the number of likes the pin has received from others, the number of repins, or the comments that pin has received.

Figure 7-14: The default "Profile" screen.

Figure 7-15: View a list of your boards on the Pinterest app.

As you navigate deeper within the sections of the app, it sometimes remembers your last point for each of the bottom menu items even if you close and reopen the app. If you tap one and find you're not, for example, on the main Profile screen, simply tap the Profile tab a second time to return to that main screen.

Tap the Likes tab to see the pins you recently liked. (See Figure 7-16.) Tap on a pin to see its original pin page.

Tap the Profile tab to go back to your main Profile page. Notice that to the right of your profile picture at the top of the screen are two buttons, one for Followers and one for Following. Tap the Followers button to see a list of followers, as shown in Figure 7-17.

Here are some of the things you can do in this list:

✔ **You can scroll up and down to see more of your followers.**

✔ **To the right of the names, you see an Unfollow button if you're already following them back.** You can tap the Unfollow button to unfollow that member.

✔ **If you're not currently following someone, you see a Follow button that you can tap to follow the person and all of their boards.** You can also tap the person's profile picture or his name to go directly to his profile page.

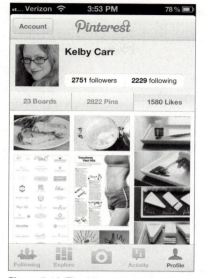

Figure 7-16: The Likes tab displays your recently liked pins.

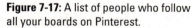

Figure 7-17: A list of people who follow all your boards on Pinterest.

Once again, tap the Profile tab to go back to your main Profile page. Now tap the Following button to see a list of the people you're following. (See Figure 7-18.)

Figure 7-18: A list of people you're following.

This list functions the same way as the Followers list, allowing you to unfollow or tap through to see their profiles.

At the risk of sounding like a broken record, tap the Profile tab one last time to return to your main Profile page. Just above your profile picture is the Account button. Tap this button and you're presented with four choices: Logout, Install Bookmarklet, Feedback, and Cancel. (See Figure 7-19.)

Tapping Logout is pretty self-explanatory. The Logout button logs you out of your profile on Pinterest in the app (but if you are logged in at other locations, such as the mobile site or the desktop site, this does not log you out there). If you have more than one account with Pinterest, this will be helpful to access the other account. When you tap Feedback, it generates a new e-mail to Pinterest. Tapping Cancel keeps you logged in to Pinterest and returns you to the page you were just on. The Install Bookmarklet option is a little more involved; check out the next section, where I give you all of the juicy details.

Installing the mobile bookmarklet

As I discuss in the preceding section, tapping the Account button on your main Profile page (accessed by tapping the Profile tab) presents you with four options. The most significant option is the Install

Bookmarklet button. (For information on the other three options, see the previous section.) The bookmarklet — which is similar to the Pin It button (see Chapter 3) you use on your home computer — it allows you to pin from your iPhone's Safari browser, and using this bookmarklet is currently the only way to do that.

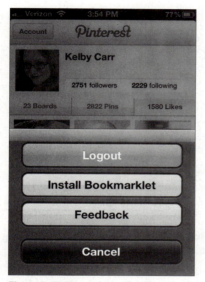

Figure 7-19: The choices presented after you click the Account button.

Installing the bookmarklet may seem a bit complicated. In fact, the Pinterest instructions even state: "As soon as this can be made simpler, it will be." If you take it one step at a time, however, it really isn't too difficult.

It's worth the couple of minutes it takes to add the bookmarklet because once you have it you'll be able to create original pins from the web. Without it, you can only repin others' pins from the web or share the photos that you take on your iPhone or that already exist on your iPhone.

To install the mobile bookmarklet, follow these instructions:

1. **Launch the Pinterest app and tap the icon for the Profile tab.**

2. **Tap the Account button and then tap the Install Bookmarklet button.**

    The iPhone's Safari opens to a page with instructions (the top of which are shown in Figure 7-20).

Figure 7-20: Instructions for installing the bookmarklet.

3. **Using your Safari bookmarks, bookmark the page with the instructions.**

   You do so by tapping the center icon (the one with a box and an arrow) in the menu on the bottom of the screen. Tap Add Bookmark and then tap Save.

4. **The next step in the instructions includes a series of text to copy. Tap inside the box with the text and then tap and hold to launch the select/paste prompt.**

5. **Tap Select All.**

6. **Tap Copy.**

7. **Tap Done.**

8. **Tap the bookmarks icon (the one that looks like an open book) in the menu on the bottom of the screen.**

9. **Tap the Edit button at the bottom-left corner of the screen and scroll down until you see the Pin It bookmark. (See Figure 7-21.)**

10. **Tap where it says Pin It.**

    You're taken to the Edit Bookmark screen, as shown in Figure 7-22.

11. **Tap the second spot down where you can edit the URL for the bookmark.**

12. **Tap the *x* to the right to clear the field and then tap and hold inside the field.**

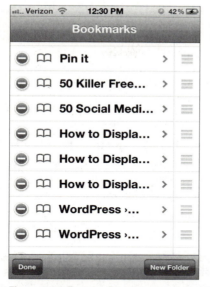

Figure 7-21: Find the Pin It bookmark to edit.

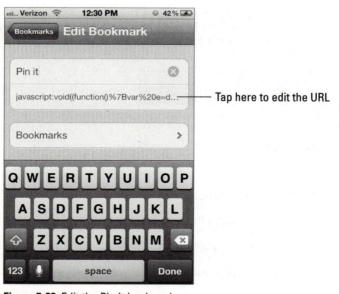

Tap here to edit the URL

Figure 7-22: Edit the Pin It bookmark.

13. **Tap Paste.**

14. **Tap Done to save your changes.**

After you install the bookmarklet, you can pin from any website in your Safari browser.

To pin from Safari, navigate to a site you want to pin as you would normally browse the Internet on your iPhone. When you're on a page with an image you want to pin, follow these steps:

1. **Tap the bookmarks icon (it looks like an open book) in the menu on the bottom of the screen.**

2. **Find the Pin It bookmark and tap it. (See Figure 7-23.)**

   On your screen, you see images from that site. (See Figure 7-24.) You may have to scroll up and down on the page to see all of the images.

3. **Tap the image you want to pin.**

   The Add a Pin screen appears.

4. **Type a description, choose a board to pin the image to, and opt to post to Facebook and Twitter.**

5. **Tap the Pin It button in the top-right corner of the screen to pin your item successfully.**

   You see the status bar at the top of the Pinterest app home screen as the pin is added, followed by a black box that says Pinned when it's completed.

Figure 7-23: Find the Pin It bookmark.

Figure 7-24: Choose an image to pin from the site.

Using Pinterest on iPad and Other Tablets

Although you can use the Pinterest iPhone app on an iPad, it isn't ideal, and there isn't yet a native iPad app, though I expect one will be available in the future. You can still download the Pinterest iPhone app and use it on the iPad, but be aware that you must either view it half screen or double-sized and pixelated. On Android and other tablets, no official Pinterest app is available.

The good news is you can use Pinterest in your tablet browser, and it functions fundamentally as it does on a desktop or laptop computer's standard browser. (See the home page as it appears on an iPad in Figure 7-25.)

You can also opt to use the mobile version of Pinterest, which you can reach at `http://m.pinterest.com` if your web browser doesn't automatically take you there when you visit Pinterest.

If you're taken directly to the Pinterest mobile site and prefer the desktop version of the site, tap your profile picture in the top-right corner of the screen and then tap the Full Site option in the drop-down menu that appears.

Figure 7-25: The Pinterest desktop site on iPad.

While you can use the desktop version of the site on your tablet to use most of the functions you would have on your computer, some key differences exist. In most instances, these differences will have little impact on your experience. For example:

- ✔ On Android tablets, you can't tap a pin from a page of pins and then use the pop-up buttons to repin, like, or comment — it automatically takes you to the pin page.

- ✔ Rearranging boards doesn't work on the iPad or on Android tablets.

Navigating the Pinterest Mobile Site

The Pinterest mobile site can be used on any tablet or smartphone running any operating system (iOS, Android, and so on) as long as the device has touchscreen capabilities. The interface of the Pinterest mobile site is straightforward with very few options, as you can see in Figure 7-26.

The Pinterest mobile site allows for searching, repinning, commenting, and liking, as well as viewing your profile or switching to the full desktop site.

To use the mobile site, visit `http://m.pinterest.com`. Alternatively, go to `www.pinterest.com` on a mobile device, and it will (in most cases) automatically take you to the mobile version of the site. Tap Login to sign in via your Facebook or Twitter account or your Pinterest account e-mail and password.

Figure 7-26: The Pinterest mobile site.

When you log in, you see the main page of the Pinterest mobile site. The main page features the most recent pins from those you follow. You can scroll down to see more. When you get to the end, you can tap Load More Pins to see more.

Each pin has Comment, Like, and Repin button below it, as shown in Figure 7-27.

To repin, tap the Repin button. A pop-up box appears, and you can choose the board to pin to, a spot to edit the description of the pin, and the option to post to Twitter if you have Twitter integrated with your Pinterest account. (See Figure 7-28.)

You can tap the Comment button below a pin to leave a comment, and you can tap the Like button to like a pin.

You can also tap the pinner's profile picture or name above any pin to view that member's profile. (Figure 7-29 shows a member's profile screen.)

From a Pinterest member's profile screen, you can tap to go directly to her website, Facebook profile, or Twitter profile (if the user has added those to her Pinterest profile). You can also scroll down to see her latest pins and likes, her followers and who she follows, and a list of her boards.

Figure 7-27: Options for pins on the Pinterest mobile site.

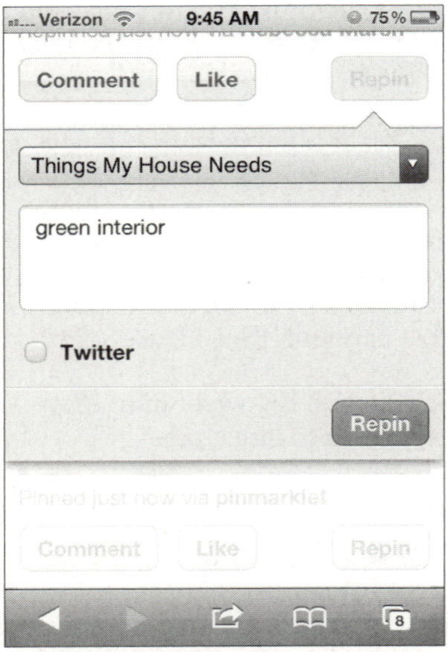

Figure 7-28: Repin from the mobile site.

Figure 7-29: Click from a pin to get to a person's profile.

From the Pinterest mobile site's profile screen, you can also tap the board name to the top-right of any pin to view that. (See Figure 7-30.)

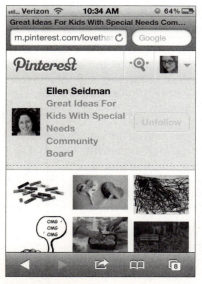

Figure 7-30: Click from a pin to a board.

At the top of any of the Pinterest mobile site's screens, you see the Search icon (it looks like a magnifying glass) just to the right of the Pinterest logo. Tap the Search icon to perform a search or to display the menu that you typically see in the top center of the screen of the desktop version of the site (including Pinners You Follow, Everything, Videos, Popular, and Gifts.). See Figure 7-31 for the drop-down menu that appears when you tap the Search icon.

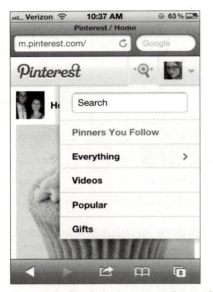

Figure 7-31: The Search menu on the mobile site.

The first option in the Search menu is the Search field. You can enter any term here to search Pinterest and then tap Go or the Enter button from your mobile browser's keyboard. The default results are searches for pins with the term in the pin's description.

In Figure 7-32, you can see that a pin icon appears above the search results along with a board icon and a person icon. The pin icon is red, indicating that the search results currently being displayed are for pins. To view the search results for boards, tap the board icon — note that the board icon now becomes red. Tap the person icon to view the search results for people — the person icon is now red.

The second option in the Search menu is Pinners You Follow, and it's the same as the default home page when you're logged in to Pinterest's mobile site. Tapping this option displays the latest pins from the people you follow.

Figure 7-32: Pin search results.

The third option in the Search drop-down menu is Everything. Tap Everything to view all the latest pins or to browse by category. You can view more categories by dragging the menu up or down to scroll. (See Figure 7-33.)

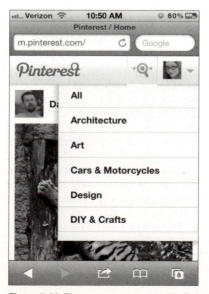

Figure 7-33: The category menu under Everything.

When you select All or any specific category to browse, you see
a screen similar to the home page with recent pins in reverse
chronological order. The top of the screen shows the category you
selected. (See Figure 7-34.)

Figure 7-34: Category pin results.

The fourth option in the Search drop-down menu is Videos. Tapping
this option displays a list of recent videos that were pinned. In my
testing, videos won't play on the iPhone or iPad. (In fact, they crash
the browsers every time during multiple attempts.) On Android
smartphones and tablets, however, the videos did play.

The fifth option in the Search drop-down menu is Popular. The Popular option displays popular pins. The final option in the Search drop-down menu is Gifts. Tap Gifts to view recent pins with a price tag label. The Popular list includes pins that have a high number of repins, likes, and comments.

There's no option to filter gifts by price range like there is on the desktop version of the site.

Tap your profile picture in the top-right corner of the screen to see three options: Profile, Full Site, and Log Out.

Tap Profile to see your Pinterest profile. You can view your icons linking to your website, Twitter profile, or Facebook profile if those are integrated into Pinterest, as well as your pins, likes, followers, following, and boards. (See Figure 7-35.)

Figure 7-35: View your profile on the Pinterest mobile site.

You can tap Full Site to view the desktop version of Pinterest on your mobile device. You can also tap Log Out to sign off of Pinterest.

Understanding Limitations of Mobile Pinterest

The Pinterest app and the mobile site provide great resources for using Pinterest on the go, but the fact remains that by nature they're more restrictive.

In some ways, the simplicity of the mobile variations makes them ideal for someone new to Pinterest. With fewer bells and whistles, the site becomes easier to navigate and use. The mobile versions also make it easy to find time to use Pinterest because you can carry the site with you anywhere.

Still, many features work poorly or are more cumbersome to do on the mobile version, such as the following:

- ✔ **Creating original pins from the web:** This is possible in some instances, but it requires extra steps. You can do this on the desktop version of the site, but not the mobile version or the app.

- ✔ **Viewing video:** This is currently impossible on iPhone and iPad whether on mobile or desktop mode, and on other phones the video is rather small.

- ✔ **Editing and revising your profile:** You can't edit and revise your profile on the mobile version or the app.

- ✔ **Rearranging boards:** You can't rearrange your boards on either mobile versions and the app nor the desktop version.

- ✔ **Adding categories to boards:** You can't add categories to boards unless you're in desktop mode.

- ✔ **Adding people to boards:** Although you can add people to boards, you must go into the desktop version of the site (not the mobile site) to do so.

If you encounter difficulties while doing tasks that you can do on your computer with Pinterest, go to the full site instead of the mobile site. Although it's awkward at times to navigate the full site on a mobile device, the full site does have more options. You can return to the mobile version of the site when you're done by typing **m.pinterest.com** into the browser address bar.

Chapter 8

Understanding Pinterest Etiquette

. . . .

In This Chapter

▶ Finding out about pin etiquette

▶ Making a quality pin

▶ Staying away from too much self-promotion

▶ Recognizing your sources

▶ Steering clear of copyright infringement

▶ Telling Pinterest about spam and inappropriate pins and members

. . . .

*P*interest is a fun site that makes it easy to share content, but with that comes a number of pitfalls. You can pin in such a way as to annoy other members, which could lose you followers or get you reported. You can also, even unwittingly, violate someone's copyright, which could potentially lead to a host of problems. By following some simple guidelines, you can be an active and responsible participant in Pinterest.

Understanding Pin Etiquette

A great place to start being an active and responsible Pinterest member is in Pinterest itself. From the home page, follow these steps:

1. **Click the About link in the top middle of the page and then choose Help from the drop-down menu.**

2. **On the Pinterest Help page that appears, click the Pin Etiquette option from the list of topics on the left.**

   A page with general Pinterest etiquette guidelines appears, as shown in Figure 8-1.

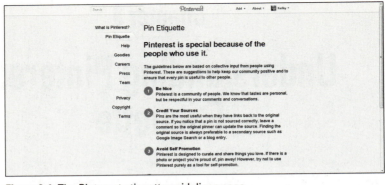

Figure 8-1: The Pinterest etiquette guidelines page.

Here are some of the highlights of the Pinterest guidelines:

✔ **Be nice.** This one's pretty self-explanatory, but with the ability to make rude comments in pin descriptions or in comments, this is a helpful tip. Although it's sometimes easy to be snarky online, keep in mind to say only things you would say directly to someone's face. Also, remember that what you say online stays online (and can be seen by anyone, including your family or your boss), so commenting in the heat of the moment may not be a good idea.

✔ **Credit your sources.** I go into this in more detail in the "Crediting Sources" section later in this chapter, but know that any image you didn't take yourself should be credited in some fashion.

✔ **Limit your self-promotion.** Yes, you can do some self-promotion on Pinterest — just be sure it's in the minority of your pins and not the majority. I cover using Pinterest for self-promotion in detail in Chapter 10, but a good general guideline is to make sure that no more than 10 percent of your pins are self-promotional.

✔ **Report objectionable content.** Pinterest doesn't want members to pin nude or obscene photos or hateful content or comments. If you see such pins, a great way to be an active and responsible member of Pinterest is to let the Pinterest team know. I cover how to do this in the "Reporting Spam and Inappropriate Pins" section later in this chapter.

✔ **Tell the Pinterest team how to make Pinterest better.** If something's driving you crazy on Pinterest, remember that the Pinterest team members want your feedback so they can provide everyone with a great experience. You can politely

share any feedback or suggestions. Keep in mind that it takes
time for changes to be implemented, and some changes aren't
feasible. Also, don't take it personally if you don't get a reply
back. The e-mail address for feedback is widely publicized
and likely receives a high volume of messages, but it's also
likely that your message will still be read and taken into consideration. You can contact Pinterest with feedback at `hi@`
`pinterest.com`.

I've also observed and heard about some behaviors from many
other members that annoy them. If you're trying to socialize, the
last thing you want to do is aggravate the community. It can cause
people to unfollow you or report your account.

Here are just a few ways to avoid annoying and alienating other
Pinterest users:

✓ **Pin from the original source.** In many cases, users create
pins from Google image results or sites such as Tumblr (a
social site where people commonly share images they find on
the web) that are clearly not the original source of the image
content. When you see an image you like in Google image
search results, for example, click through the image in Google
to find the original website where the image appears. You can
click through and find the original site by clicking the image
in Google results and then clicking the Website for This Image
link (as you can see in the top-right corner of Figure 8-2). Pin
from the site that is the original source of the image instead of
another social sharing or search site.

Click this link

Figure 8-2: Find the original source for a Google Image result.

✔ **Pin the deep link to the content.** If you're on a site's main page, be sure you click headlines for posts to find the *deep link* (as you can see in Figure 8-3), or *permalink,* where the post will always be located. This tip is especially important on blogs, where the latest posts are always originally posted on the home page but then move off the home page as new content is created.

Click a headline to go to the deep link

Figure 8-3: Find a post's headline on a blog to click through to the permalink.

✔ **Describe what's in the pin clearly.** Using descriptions like "need this" or "yummy" are off-putting to people who see only your description and the image. Instead, your pin descriptions should say what's in the image from the original source. For example, instead of "yummy," say "chicken and rice recipe." Out of context, some images can be hard to identify without a clear description, especially food dishes that may not be as identifiable from the image alone.

✔ **Don't over-share.** If you're pinning, be careful to use the description only to briefly describe the pin. Don't copy and paste the entire content, post, article, or page where it's originally located — this is rude to the original content creator, and it's also a copyright violation. This is commonly seen with craft instructions and recipes. In response to this, Pinterest now limits descriptions to 500 characters.

✔ **Pin from the source on the web so the pin will link to the source.** Don't download an image from a website and then upload it to Pinterest — if you do it that way, people can't find the source because this method doesn't automatically include a link to the source where you found the image. Besides being a copyright issue, it's also annoying to anyone who wants more information about the pin.

✔ **If you're uploading a photo, make sure you took the photo.** Don't save photos that belong to others and pin them. It can also be helpful to make it clear in the pin description that you took the photo so no one reports you for copyright infringement.

✔ **Don't blatantly self-promote yourself in every pin.** I've seen some users who include a link to their profile or a link to their own website in every pin they make. This is a quick way to lose followers and seem far too pushy and sales-oriented.

✔ **Avoid pinning or repinning in too rapid of a fashion on one very targeted topic.** It's fine to have very specific pins, but when you create several pins on the same topic in a matter of seconds, the pins will hit your followers' streams and take over. If someone isn't interested in purple shoes and you pin ten of them in a row to your Favorite Purple Shoes board, it could result in people choosing to unfollow you so they get more diverse pins in their stream.

Creating a Quality Pin

A *quality pin* is easy to repin, clearly states the content of the pin, links back to the source if it's pinned from the web, and is interesting enough to be worthy of a repin. Most of all, a quality pin includes an image that's eye-catching and engaging.

Here are some tips for building a quality pin:

✔ **Find a quality image to pin.** Images that are too small (below 240 pixels on either side) don't look good in the stream because they can end up smaller than the other thumbnails. The image should also be visually interesting and aesthetically pleasing. The content of the image should be clear.

✔ **When pinning from the web, pin from interesting sources with quality content.** Yes, a great image might look good on your board, but people like to click through and find something helpful. For example, it's better for an image of a do-it-yourself (DIY) project to link to an article with a detailed tutorial rather than a page that merely has an image and very little detail about it. An image of a great food dish, like the one shown in Figure 8-4, is better if it's linked to a recipe instead of an image with very little explanation of how to make it.

✔ **Be clear and concise in your pin description.** Using your pin descriptions to state what's in the image can actually be an important factor in whether your pin is repinned. If you're repinning someone else's image, take the time to read their description and modify it if necessary (especially if they share

an entire post, have an unclear description, or personalize
their description in a way that doesn't make sense coming
from you). If the pin is a how-to, tutorial, recipe, and so on,
say that in the description.

Figure 8-4: A quality pin that clearly describes the content and
links to a website with a recipe.

If you're pinning your own image directly, it's even more
important to write a clear description of the image. Let people
know that you took the picture and say clearly what it is and
where you took it (if applicable to the image).

You can include a URL in a description to link to more information,
even if you're pinning an image directly. For example, if you pin an
image of a delicious dish from a restaurant, you can include the
restaurant's website URL to help people find out more about the
eatery.

There are many subtle nuances (sometimes it's a matter of a really
funny or emotional image, sometimes it's really helpful tutorials
and how-to's, and sometimes it's just a pretty picture) to what's
popular or engaging in a pin. Experiment to find out which pins get
repinned the most.

Avoiding Too Much Self-Promotion

Pinterest has been the focus of quite a bit of news, online coverage, and social media buzz. Part of the reason for this is people
are discovering Pinterest drives a lot of traffic to websites via the
source URLs for pins.

Using Pinterest to drive traffic to websites can make it tempting to jump into Pinterest and dedicate most of your pins to sharing your own content for the sole purpose of self-promotion. Not only is this bad etiquette, but it's not effective. The odds are good that if you only promote yourself, people will not follow you, they will unfollow you if they're already following you, they will not repin you, and they will not click through your pins to your content.

That said, you can promote your own content. Do it sparingly, however, and be sure that you pin or repin other people's content quite a bit between each pin of your own content. You can also create a board for your own self-promotional content (as you can see a member has done in Figure 8-5).

Figure 8-5: This board identifies self-promotional pins.

The nice thing about creating a board for your own self-promotion is it clearly tells your followers a pin is self-promotional, which is good for disclosure and shouldn't annoy anyone unless you do self-promotional pins in rapid-fire fashion. Having such a board also makes it easy for someone who is interested in your self-promoting pins to find them all in one place with ease.

Crediting Sources

Because the Pinterest platform revolves around sharing content, it's crucial to be careful about crediting the source properly. When it comes to pinning from the web, the solution is simple in theory. You need not add a credit in the description for a pin that's generated from a website because the pin automatically links directly to the source you used. The pin's individual page cites the source domain, as you can see in Figure 8-6 just above and to the left of the pin.

Figure 8-6: The source of a pin is listed just above and to the left of it.

Just be sure to follow the advice earlier in this chapter and ensure you find the original, credible source for the content and image, and be sure you pin directly from that source.

If you happen to know the person who is the source of the content you're pinning and you follow one another on Pinterest, you can also tag the member in the pin description by typing @ and then entering the person's name. (See Chapter 5 for more about tagging Pinterest members.) This works on the desktop site, but not the mobile site or the mobile app.

For images that you upload directly from your hard drive or mobile device, in all likelihood you own the image so this shouldn't be an issue. If you're uploading an image that features something that can also be found online, it can be considerate and helpful to your followers to include the full URL (http://pinterest.com, for example) in the description. That will become a working link on the pin page.

Avoiding Copyright Infringement

As with any site that allows its members to share, bookmark, and curate what's on the web, copyright infringement is a concern. When you're using Pinterest, a good guideline is to be respectful of content owned by others. Don't copy an article or post it in its entirety to use in a description, as that's the intellectual property of the original content creator.

There's a common misconception that content on the web is all in the public domain. On the contrary, any content that's published should be assumed to be protected by copyright. It's allowable as "fair use," which allows for brief excerpts of content to be quoted, to use in a pin description a quote or short excerpt from someone else's copyrighted content. You can't, however, copy the bulk (or even a large portion) of the content.

Although there's no exact rule on a number of words or a percentage of content that defines fair use, a great guideline is to ask yourself whether someone would have to click through your pin to the original content to find out all they need to know. If they wouldn't need to click through — meaning your pin captures the entire essence of the post or the article — then you've included too much information in your pin description.

If you don't want people to pin images your site, you can find instructions to block people from pinning by visiting the Pinterest home page, mousing over About, clicking Help, and scrolling down to click where it says, "What if I don't want images from my site to be pinned?" This will get a snippet of code that you can add to block pinning of images from your site.

A great resource on copyright law is the U.S. Copyright Office's site at `http://copyright.gov`, which includes the entire U.S. copyright law, tip sheets, downloadable brochures (such as the Copyright Basics one in Figure 8-7), and an FAQ page.

Figure 8-7: The U.S. Copyright Office's online brochure, Copyright Basics.

Reporting Spam and Inappropriate Pins

If you see pins that are inappropriate, clearly spam (keeping in mind some self-promotion is expected so long as it's tasteful), hateful, obscene, or a copyright violation, you can report them to Pinterest. Although a single self-promotional pin is okay, for example, someone who quickly and repeatedly pins images to sell you something is spamming.

Although there's no option to report a member or a board at this time, you can report any pin. To do so, just follow these steps:

1. **Go directly to the pin page you want to report.**

2. **To the right of the pin are several options; click the Report Pin button. (See Figure 8-8.)**

Click this button

Figure 8-8: The Report Pin button on a pin page.

The Report Pin dialog box appears with several options for reasons you are reporting the pin.

3. **Click to select the radio button next to your reason for reporting the pin. (See Figure 8-9.)**

You may click to select Other for a reason not listed and complete the space for comments if you would like.

Figure 8-9: Report a pin.

4. Click the Report Pin button.

If you own copyright of the material in the pin, there's also a link just to the right of the Report Pin submission button to click for information on reporting copyright infringement. Several people have reported that they've taken these steps and seen the copyrighted material removed very quickly (including the original pin of their copyrighted image and all repins that came later).

Chapter 9

Controlling Privacy and Other Settings

*Y*es, Pinterest is a social network, but that doesn't mean you necessarily want to share everything (or everywhere) or have your e-mail inbox overrun with constant notifications. The advice I give people regularly regarding all social networks and the Internet is just as applicable here. Don't say something online unless you're comfortable with anyone being able to see it: your parents, your children, your boss, your spouse, or strangers.

If something is online on Pinterest (or on any other site, for that matter), anyone can potentially find it. Even if you tighten settings, such as keeping your profile out of search results, people may still be able to find profiles and pins by using methods outside of search engines.

The interesting thing about Pinterest is that people seem more relaxed about their sharing than on other social networks. For example, I've noticed people who I never see use expletives else-where online pin quotes with them on Pinterest. Whatever your comfort level is for sharing, just be aware that Pinterest is still a public site.

Understanding the Pinterest Privacy Policy

It can be helpful to understand the privacy policy of a site you use regularly, especially one where you are socially sharing. You can read the entire policy on the Pinterest site. Luckily, I did it for you so you don't have to scour the fine print and boring legalese. If you do need to find the full policy, go to the Pinterest home page, click the About link in the top-middle area of the screen, and choose Help from the drop-down menu. On the Help page, click the Privacy link in the left column to view and read the Pinterest Privacy Policy. (See Figure 9-1.)

Figure 9-1: The Pinterest privacy policy.

 Keep in mind that websites can change their privacy policy at any time, and social networks are known for doing that regularly. I suggest checking the Pinterest Privacy Policy periodically to be sure you're familiar with any changes the site has made.

Here's a summary of the key points from the policy:

✔ **Collection of personal information:** When you register with Pinterest, you connect it with another social network (Facebook and/or Twitter), and Pinterest accesses and collects some of your profile information from that network when you become a Pinterest member. This is quite common, and websites such as Pinterest do that to easily collect registration information without forcing people to manually enter it.

Pinterest doesn't intentionally collect information on children under age 13, and any parent who believes his or her child's information has been collected can e-mail hi@pinterest. com to report it and have it deleted. Clearly, it would be difficult for Pinterest to individually confirm all members are over this age, but the site doesn't seek out children as members and will respond if a parent discovers this.

✔ **Use of personal information:** Pinterest uses your profile information to contact you through methods such as an e-mail newsletter, but you can unsubscribe from that at any time through the instructions in any e-mail newsletter or in your Pinterest e-mail settings (described in the "Reducing E-Mail from Pinterest" section later in this chapter).

✔ **Profile information that's shared:** When you set up your profile, some of the information you use (such as your name, your picture, and your website if you add that to your profile settings) is made visible on Pinterest and is thus shared with others. Other details, such as your e-mail address, are not.

✔ **Use of cookies on Pinterest:** The site uses *cookies,* which are bits of data that are collected when you visit a site (for example, to remember your login information). The use of cookies is a common practice for websites when you browse the Internet. You can adjust your browser settings so cookies aren't allowed, but some of the functions of the site may not work properly if you do.

✔ **Sharing via Facebook or Facebook Connect:** Members have the option to share their activity on Facebook via Facebook Connect. This can be disabled even once enabled, but while it's enabled, your pins and other actions on Pinterest will appear on your Facebook Wall (as you can see in Figure 9-2).

Pinterest activity appears here

Figure 9-2: Pinterest activity on a Facebook Wall.

✔ **Personal information may be archived:** If you delete or change your Pinterest account profile, Pinterest might keep the information in its archives if required by law or for business purposes.

Keeping Your Account Out of Google Search

One way to increase your privacy on Pinterest is to set your profile so it doesn't appear in Google Search. For most people, there's no reason for this setting (and, in fact, it's counterproductive to getting more exposure on Pinterest), but it is available as an option.

Although this setting will cut back on public and nonmember views of your profile, remember that people can still find many other pathways to find your profile and content on Pinterest. Don't assume your account will be private just because you use this setting — it won't be.

To keep your profile out of Google Search, follow these instructions:

1. **Log in to your Pinterest account and mouse over your name in the top-right corner.**

   A drop-down menu appears.

2. **Choose the Settings option.**

   The Edit Profile page appears.

3. **Scroll down until you see Visibility section and click the slider to change it to On to hide your profile from search engines. (See Figure 9-3.)**

   The default for the Visibility option is Off. Changing the slider to On hides your Pinterest profile from search engines.

4. **At the bottom of the page, click the Save Profile button.**

Reducing E-Mail from Pinterest

It's nice to know when you get new followers or someone repins, likes, or comments on something you've pinned. As hard as e-mail can be to wrangle these days, however, you might want to cut down on the volume.

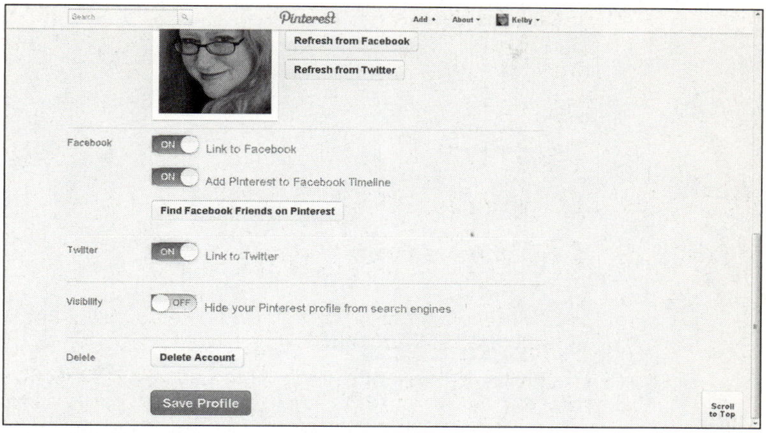

Figure 9-3: The Visibility option under Settings.

Fortunately, Pinterest allows you to customize how much or how little e-mail you receive. In fact, you can opt to receive no e-mail and instead see activity on your profile and pins directly on the site. For more on your Pinterest profile settings, see Chapter 1.

To adjust your e-mail settings, follow these steps:

1. **Log in to your Pinterest account and mouse over your name in the top-right corner of the screen.**

   A drop-down menu appears.

2. **Choose the Settings option.**

   The Edit Profile page appears.

3. **Click the Change Email Settings button.**

   It's the second option on the page, as shown in Figure 9-4.

   The Email Settings page appears.

4. **Adjust the settings to reflect your preferences.**

   As shown in Figure 9-5, you can change a variety of options including:

   • You can turn e-mail notifications on or off.

   • You can set how often you receive e-mails (immediately for more e-mails or a daily summary for fewer e-mails).

   • You can select the check boxes for the notifications you want to receive.

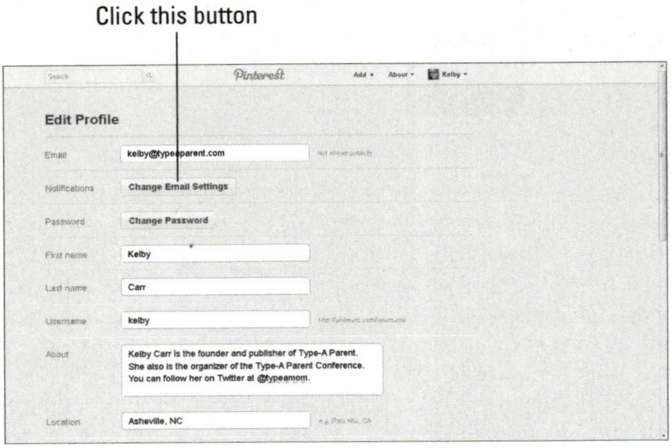

Click this button

Figure 9-4: The Change Email Settings button on the Edit Profile page.

You can always come back and change your settings later if you decide you're getting too many or too few e-mails.

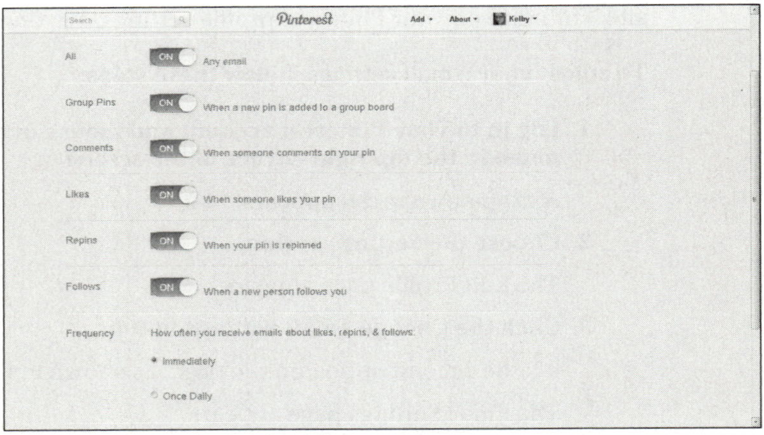

Figure 9-5: The e-mail options available on Pinterest.

5. **Scroll to the bottom of the page and click the Save Settings button.**

If you aren't receiving e-mails, check your e-mail program's spam folder. If you find that any e-mails from Pinterest landed there, alert your e-mail provider that it's not spam.

Controlling Social Sharing When You Pin

The ability to share your pins (even as you pin) on Facebook and Twitter is handy. If you have Pinterest integrated into your Facebook Timeline (as mentioned earlier in Chapter 1), all your activity on Pinterest automatically appears on your Facebook Wall (even pins you don't specifically share on Facebook). However, because it happens behind the scenes, it can be easy to forget that your activity is being publically displayed on Facebook.

If you use Pinterest in your Facebook Timeline, a section of your Wall will list your latest pins, repins, comments, and likes. If you like a pin, it creates a new update on your Facebook Wall with a thumbnail of the pin and basic information about it. If you tweet a pin, you'll post an update to your Twitter profile with a link to the pin and basic information about the pin.

In most cases, this visible activity isn't a major issue, because you're already sharing publicly online. If it is a concern, however, you can disable the Facebook or Twitter sharing, as well as the automated posting of all you Pinterest activity to your Facebook Timeline on your Wall.

You are required by Pinterest to have one social network (either Facebook or Twitter) connected to your Pinterest profile in order to log in to your Pinterest account.

To adjust these social network connections, follow these instructions:

1. **Log in to your Pinterest account and mouse over your name in the top-right corner of the screen.**

   A drop-down menu appears.

2. **Choose the Settings option.**

   The Edit Profile Page appears.

3. **Scroll down the page and locate the area with the Facebook and Twitter settings. (See Figure 9-6.)**

4. **Click the slider On or Off for linking Facebook, depending on your preference.**

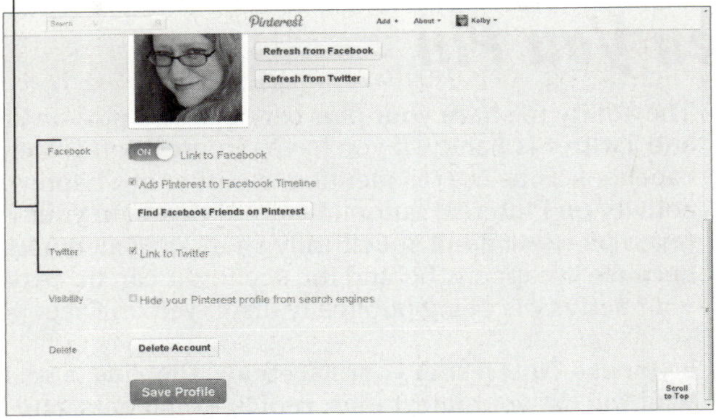

Facebook and Twitter settings

Figure 9-6: Facebook and Twitter settings on the Edit Profile page.

5. **If you've integrated Facebook with your Pinterest account, you can also click the slider On or Off for the Add Pinterest to Facebook Timeline option.**

If you want to have the ability to share certain pins manually on Facebook without the automated sharing of all activity, keep Facebook linked but click the slider to Off for the Add Pinterest to Facebook Timeline option.

6. **Click the slider On or Off to link to your Twitter profile, depending on your preference.**

7. **Click the Save Profile button at the bottom of the page.**

Even the manual sharing on Facebook and Twitter can easily happen without you noticing as you do it. The Pin It bookmarklet and mobile app both remember your last share settings. If your last pin was shared to Facebook (or Twitter), the next one will also be shared to Facebook (or Twitter) unless you change your settings.

You might want to share one pin on other social networks, and then repin several others and fail to notice the Facebook or Twitter sharing is still checked as on. It's something to keep in mind as you pin.

Changing Your Username

You can change your username on Pinterest if you decide the one you chose when you registered isn't a good fit. It's a simple process.

Your Pinterest profile's URL format is `http://pinterest.com/`
USERNAME. If you change your username, that will also change the
URL to your profile, so proceed with caution. Anywhere you've
linked your profile, anyone who has bookmarked your profile, and
anyone else who links to your profile will get an error when they go
to the old URL. If you do change your username, be sure to update
any links to your profile with the new URL and share the new URL
with anyone that you know has linked to your profile. If anyone has
linked to your profile and you aren't aware of the link, or if someone isn't willing to update the URL to your profile, the link will be
broken.

To change your username, follow these steps:

1. **Log in to your Pinterest account and mouse over your
   name in the top-right corner of the screen.**

   A drop-down menu appears.

2. **Choose the Settings option.**

   The Edit Profile Page appears.

3. **Scroll down and locate the Username field. (See Figure 9-7.)**

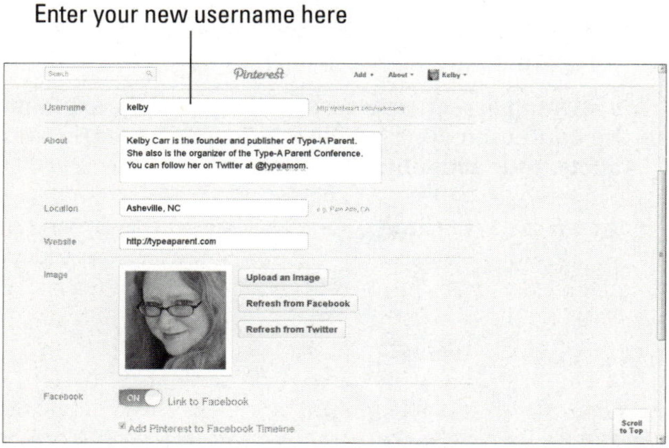

Enter your new username here

Figure 9-7: Changing your username.

4. **Type a new username in the text box.**

   Note that you can't leave spaces or include special characters in your username.

5. **Scroll to the bottom of the page and click the Save Profile
   button.**

Deactivating Your Account

In rare instances, you might want to delete your Pinterest account entirely. For example, you might have more than one account and want to get rid of the one that you don't use.

If you're deleting an account to concentrate on a new profile instead, you can go into the profile that's on the chopping block and repin or like any pins you want to save before you delete the account.

Before you delete your account, be aware there is no turning back. When you delete the account, all pins and boards are permanently deleted from Pinterest.

To delete your Pinterest account, follow these steps:

1. **Log in to your Pinterest account and mouse over your name in the top-right corner of the screen.**

   A drop-down menu appears.

2. **Choose the Settings option.**

   The Edit Profile Page appears.

3. **Scroll down and click the Delete Account button. (See Figure 9-8.)**

   A warning screen appears (see Figure 9-9), explaining that all the content in your profile will be permanently removed if you delete your account.

Search	Pinterest Add ▾ About ▾ Kelby ▾

Website	http://typeaparent.com
Image	Type-A Parent Upload an Image
	typeaparent.com Refresh from Twitter
Facebook	OFF Link to Facebook
Twitter	ON Link to Twitter
Visibility	OFF Hide your Pinterest profile from search engines
Delete	Delete Account
	Save Profile

Click this button

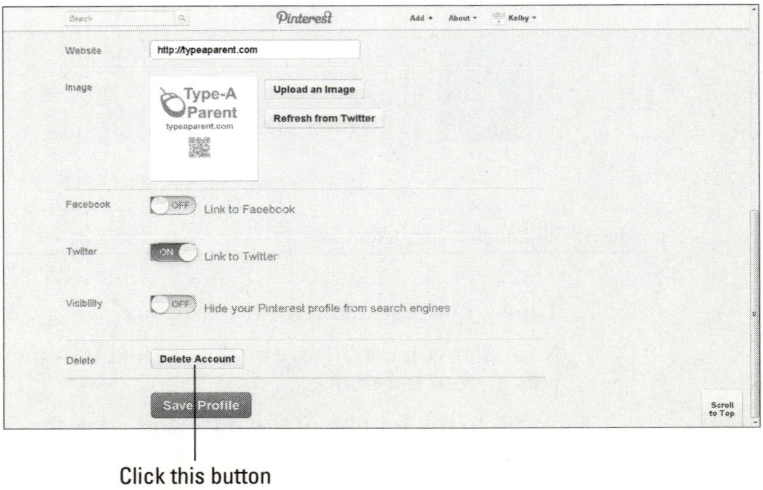

Figure 9-8: The Delete Account button.

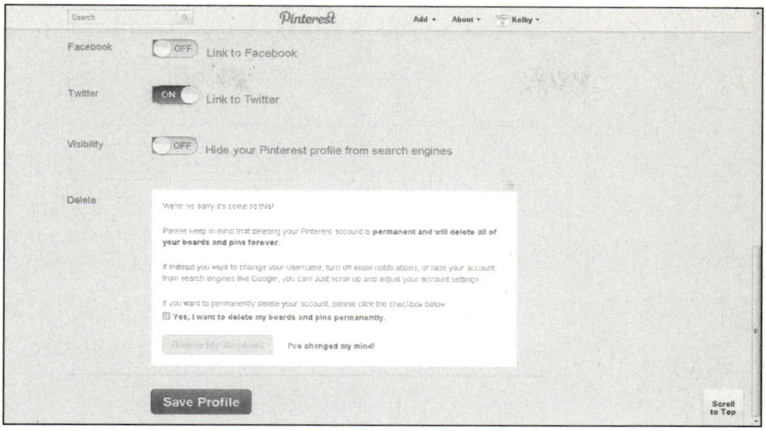

Figure 9-9: The warning before deleting your account.

4. **Select the check box labeled Yes, I Want to Delete My Pins and Boards Permanently.**

5. **Click the Delete My Account button.**

Chapter 10

Self-Promoting on Pinterest

*P*interest is fun, educational, and entertaining, but it's also a great way to promote your own site, products, or blog — if you do it appropriately. If you focus too much on self-promotion, you'll turn off potential readers, clients, and customers. If you focus too little on it, you won't accomplish your goals of gaining exposure for your own site. It's a delicate balance.

If you spend time engaging and interacting on topics of mutual interest, sprinkled with a sparse dusting of self-promotion, you'll find that Pinterest can be a powerful driver of traffic, buzz, and sales.

Finding Your Site's Pins

It's quite possible your site is already getting buzz on Pinterest, even if you just joined and haven't pinned anything from it yet. You can see what pins link to your site by typing in a URL using this format: **http://pinterest.com/source/*YOURSITE.COM***. All the recent pins originating from your site are displayed, as shown in Figure 10-1.

This shows you a list of original pins from your site, not repins. You can drill down to see repins by clicking any pin image and then looking below the pinned image on the pin page for who repinned. You can even then click those pins to see who repinned the repins.

Figure 10-1: Pins from a specific site.

This is the easiest way to find a pin from your site. As you navigate Pinterest, however, you may encounter pins from your site in the stream or on your own profile and boards. When you do, you can navigate from an image pinned from your site to the results page for all pins from your site. To do so, follow these steps:

1. **Find a pin from your site and click it to go to that specific pin page.**

   Beneath the pin image are various details about the pin, such as who liked and repined it, the board it was pinned to, and so on. You also see a header reading `Pinned via [method] from [domain]`, as shown in the bottom-right corner of Figure 10-2.

Domain source for a pin is listed here

Figure 10-2: Find the domain source for a pin.

2. **Click the domain, and you're taken to the list of pins from that site.**

Writing a Post or Page That's Pin-Worthy

Certain types of content do better than others when it comes to Pinterest sharing. How the content is set up is also a major factor. You want your content, website, or post/article to be interesting, easy to pin, and feature attractive images.

Here are the key elements to a post or page that's pin-worthy:

✔ **A great image is mandatory.** Figure 10-3 shows a page from `www.home.ec101.com` and is a great example of the kind of image content you should strive for. If you have no image at all, someone might pin your logo, but that isn't as attractive (or identifying to the content). See the "Optimizing Images for Pinning" section, later in this chapter, for more on pin-worthy images.

Figure 10-3: Content with a quality image for pinning, as well as quality content with instructions.

✔ **Great content beyond the image encourages pinning.** People want to share good articles and posts that educate, entertain, and enlighten their Pinterest followers.

✔ **Your post or page should be easy to pin, and you should remind people they can pin.** Installing a Pin It button on your website is ideal. See the "Installing the Pin It Button for Websites on Products, Posts, and Web Pages" section, later in this chapter, for all the details.

Types of content that are frequently shared on Pinterest include the following:

- ✔ Tutorials on pretty much anything, from crafts to technology
- ✔ Do-it-yourself (DIY) projects
- ✔ Organization tips and projects
- ✔ Pop culture icons such as Star Wars and Harry Potter
- ✔ Photo galleries and photo-driven content
- ✔ Recipes and food/cooking instructional content, as shown in Figure 10-4

Figure 10-4: Recipe pins on Pinterest.

- ✔ Infographics, which are statistics presented in graphic form for easy comprehension, including things such as pie and bar charts and catchy imagery
- ✔ Graphic images of quotes and sayings
- ✔ Funny pictures and phrases
- ✔ Content about Pinterest (as seen in Figure 10-5 showing my Pinterest For Dummies board), as well as other social networks
- ✔ Exercise instructional graphics
- ✔ Top Ten lists
- ✔ Products people love and recommend, especially interesting, unique, and innovative ones

Figure 10-5: My Pinterest For Dummies board with pins of content about Pinterest, located at `http://pinterest.com/pinterest-for-dummies`.

The preceding list shouldn't limit you, however. All sorts of content gets pinned, and this isn't an all-inclusive list. As long as your content is interesting and has a great image, it's pinnable.

Optimizing Images for Pinning

Not all images can be pinned to Pinterest, and some aren't likely to encourage repins. In addition, some images on your page might be displayed too small to stand out on a Pinterest board page, pin stream page, or even on the mobile version of the Pinterest site.

First of all, be sure the image on your page is even pinnable. If you use something like a plugin (an addon for a web platform to give it additional functionality) to display images on a page or a post, it may prevent the image from being pinned. You can check whether or not the images on your page or post are pinnable by going to your page or post you wish to pin, adding the URL as a pin, and seeing whether all the images appear. I have instructions on how to create a pin in Chapter 3.

Some of the instructions in this chapter might require web development knowledge or the assistance of a webmaster or a tech-savvy friend.

If some of the images on your page or post don't appear, it's typically because some sort of dynamic coding is being used to display your images. (You can't pin from Facebook, for example, as shown in Figure 10-6.)

Figure 10-6: You can't pin an image from some sites, such as Facebook.

Examine your site's plugins, addons, modules, or code for a feature that's used to display images. You may need to disable it entirely or check with that plug-in's developer for a workaround. With so many possibilities — website and blog platforms and various third-party plugins — I can't address all possibilities with instructions in these pages.

The best bet is to go to the source, such as a support forum for your website or blog platform or for the plugin itself, and ask whether anyone else is having this issue and has found a solution.

After you've verified that images on your page or post can be pinned, you need to ensure the images will display well and engage your audience on Pinterest. Here are some tips:

- ✔ **Be sure images are a minimum of 250 pixels on both sides, ideally.** Although people can pin smaller images, on Pinterest the guideline is bigger is better (while staying web-friendly and not getting so large that the image is slow to load, such as a size above 1,000 pixels on a side).

- ✔ **You might consider adding a watermark to the images you own and post that you hope will be pinned.** Adding a watermark helps gain more exposure for your site's name and also protects images if they're used without your permission elsewhere. Most image-editing programs have that option, and you can also find software available for the purpose of adding watermarks. In addition, some free websites allow you to watermark your images, such as www.picmarkr.com and www.watermarktool.com.

✔ **Consider adding text onto the image describing the content that people will find if they navigate to your site from the pin (as shown in Figure 10-7).** Adding text to an image can help encourage people to click through the image to get the information.

✔ **Some people also use collages (see Figure 10-8) with multiple images to show that the content is a tutorial, which can be enticing to those who see it in their Pinterest stream.**

Text added to an image

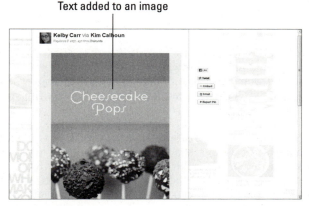

Figure 10-7: An image from a site that includes text stating what's in the content when you click through.

Figure 10-8: A collage to depict multiple images relevant to content when it's pinned.

Installing the Pin It Button for Websites on Products, Posts, and Web Pages

One of the best ways to encourage pinning of your content is to make it easy and to remind people when they're on your site to pin. Adding the Pinterest Pin It button for websites is a great way to accomplish both of those goals.

The difference between the Pin It button referenced earlier in this book at the Pin It button for websites is that the standard Pin It button is used in your browser bar to pin images you see as you browse the web. The Pin It button for websites appears on the web page itself, and it doesn't require that a user have the standard Pin It button installed in her browser.

The Pin It button for websites allows your visitors to click the button and follow a couple of steps to create a pin, behaving essentially as if they used the browser Pin It button (see Chapter 3 for instructions on how to install and use the Pinterest Pin It button). Still, the visual reminder to pin content can be powerful and motivating.

A Pin It button for websites can be displayed before or after content (or both) or alongside it. (You can see an example of a Pin It button for websites after a post at www.thecentsiblelife.com in Figure 10-9.)

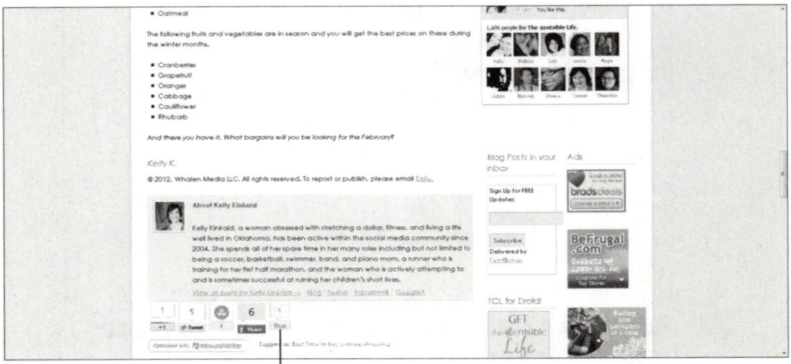

Pin It button for websites

Figure 10-9: A Pin It button for websites used after a post.

If you have a site or blog built with WordPress, you currently have a few options for using a plugin to easily add a Pin It web button for websites. (Find out more about plugins in the "Pinterest Widgets and Plugins" section later in this chapter.) Unfortunately, if your site uses any other platform, your options are more limited and require coding or using the options in this section from Pinterest.

There are a few disadvantages to the Pinterest Pin It button for websites. For one thing, you have to manually add it to every page or post you want it to appear. You also have to specify an image and can optionally add a description. That has its advantages as well, but it also takes the choice away from your site's visitors on selecting an image and forces them to edit the description to use a different one. The Pin It button for websites is also more difficult and time-consuming to add than something like a plugin that you set up once and automatically generates a pin button for all your content.

Before you follow the instructions, be sure you're logged in to Pinterest so it will generate the code specific to your profile.

To add the Pinterest Pin It button for websites, follow these steps:

1. **From the Pinterest home page, mouse over the About link and, from the drop-down menu that appears, click Pin It Button.**

   The Goodies page appears.

2. **Scroll down the page and locate the Pin It Button for Websites section. (See Figure 10-10.)**

![Screenshot of the Pinterest Goodies page showing the "Pin It" Button for Websites section with customization form fields and code]

Figure 10-10: The Pinterest instructions and code for adding a Pin It button for websites.

3. **Find and copy the URL for the blog post, article or web page you will add the code to.**

   The URL should be the deep link to that web page, not your site's home page (unless your home page is the page you're adding the button to). You can usually find the permalink for an article by clicking the title.

4. **Paste the URL in the URL of the Webpage the Pin is On field.**

5. **Find and copy the URL for the image you want people to pin that's located on the page.**

   On the page, you can find the URL for the image on a PC by right-clicking and viewing the image or right-clicking and viewing the image URL, then copying. On a Mac, you can get the image URL by pressing Ctrl while clicking the image and then choosing Copy Image Location from the options.

6. **Paste the image URL into the URL of the Image to be Pinned field.**

7. **(Optional) Type a description of the pin in the Description text box.**

   Although including a description does have disadvantages as I mention earlier, it also gives you the ability to direct what's said on Pinterest (and help avoid people copying your entire content text). A clear description here is optimal.

8. **(Optional) Use the drop-down menu in the right column to choose between a horizontal or vertical button or to display without a pin count.**

9. **Copy the code you see in the Add This Code to Your Site text box.**

10. **Paste the code in the source (not visual) editor for your page or post where you want it to appear.**

    The best locations are above and below content (or both) or right next to, above, or below the image you would like pinned.

Pinterest also offers an advanced option to allow for multiple images to be pinned on one page through the Advanced option in the code section. However, it requires more advanced knowledge of code to customize. It allows you to place the top portion of code on the page, and then an abbreviated code (at the bottom of the advanced code box) in each location you want a Pin It button. Each location can pin a different image and have a different description. You need to complete the fields for URL, image, and description for each pin to generate the code for each pin under Advanced, at the bottom after you see Customize and Include for Each Button on the Page.

Finding Pinterest Linkups and Places to Share Pins and Profiles

One way to gain followers and engagement with your Pinterest profile is to find places off of Pinterest to share your pins, boards, or profile. Such places are known as Pinterest *linkups,* and they're becoming more popular as Pinterest grows in usage. There are linkups that are weekly as well as ones that are general or specific to a topic.

An example of a weekly linkup from www.5minutesformom.com featuring pins or boards is shown in Figure 10-11. You can also find linkups to share profiles. Some regular linkups allow you to share posts you would like others to pin to Pinterest.

A Pinterest linkup

Figure 10-11: A Pin It Friday linkup at the 5 Minutes for Mom website.

Here are a few linkups where you can share your profile, Pinterest pins and boards, or posts you would like pinned:

- ✔ You can find the weekly Pin It Friday linkup at 5 Minutes for Mom at www.5minutesformom.com/category/feature-columns/pin-it-friday.

- ✔ My site features a Pinterest Profile Linkup for parents at www.typeaparent.com/pinterest-profile-linkup.html as well as regular topic and category linkups that can be found at www.typeaparent.com/tag/pinterest.

✔ You can find a weekly Friday linkup, Get Pinspired, at She Promotes at `www.shepromotes.com/tag/pinterest`.

✔ At Crafty Mama of Four, you can find the Pin Me! weekly Pinterest linkup, where you can share posts you would like linked at `www.craftymamaof4.com/tag/pinterest`.

 You can search Google for terms like *"Pinterest linkup," "Pinterest link up," "Pinterest blog hop,"* or *"Pinterest linky"* to find more link-ups, or add a topic to the search to find niche Pinterest linkups. Although there are several linkups now, I expect many more will soon be created.

Adding a Follow Me on Pinterest Button to Your Site

If you have a website or blog, a great way to gain new followers is by simply letting people know you're on Pinterest and making it easy for them to follow you there.

Pinterest provides code for a Follow Me on Pinterest button that links to your profile and Pinterest also offers size choices for the button to best fit your site. If you're using WordPress, see the next section in this chapter for a recommendation of a Follow Me on Pinterest widget plugin.

 Before you follow the instructions, be sure you're logged in to Pinterest so it will generate the code specific to your profile.

To add a Follow Me on Pinterest button, take these steps:

1. **From the home page, mouse over the About link and, from the drop-down menu that appears, choose Pin It Button.**

   The Goodies page appears.

2. **Scroll down and locate the Follow Button for Websites section. (See Figure 10-12.)**

   As you can see, Pinterest offers various options for the size and style of the button.

3. **Click the image of the button you want to use.**

   When you click the image, code is automatically generated to its right and highlighted.

4. **Copy the code.**

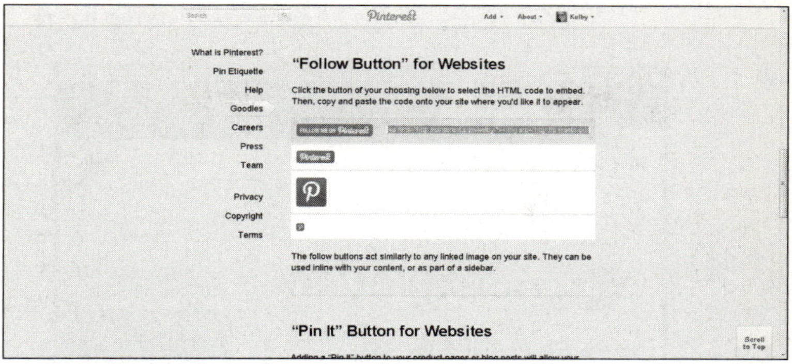

Figure 10-12: Creating a Follow Me on Pinterest button to use on your blog or website.

5. **On your website or blog, find the place to insert code (such as a sidebar), paste the code, and then save.**

   Be sure you're in a source or HTML area so that the code will render.

6. **View your site to ensure the button is showing and click the button to make sure it links to your profile on Pinterest.**

You can also find some free Pinterest icons to use or even customize a Pinterest button or logo to match your site (as shown in the top-right corner of `http://coloradomoms.com` in Figure 10-13). Be sure if you use an unofficial Pinterest icon that it's one that states it's free to download and use. You would use the image and link it to your profile URL.

Pinterest Widgets and Plugins

WordPress offers Pinterest plugins to add a Pin It button for websites (better, in my opinion, than the options via the Pinterest site mentioned in the "Installing the Pin It Button for Websites on Products, Posts, and Web Pages" section earlier in this chapter). There are also WordPress plug-ins to display your latest pins on your site or blog, which can be even more appealing for your site's visitors to click through and follow you on Pinterest.

A customized Pinterest button

Figure 10-13: A Follow Me on Pinterest button that has been designed to match a site design.

Although many options are available, some work better than others. I also expect more plug-ins to be added rapidly in the near future. To see all WordPress Pinterest-related plug-ins, visit the WordPress plug-in site and search for *Pinterest,* or visit `http://wordpress.org/extend/plugins/search. php?q=pinterest`. Be sure to look closely at ratings and read the reviews of plug-ins.

I recommend three of the WordPress plug-ins that are currently available:

✔ To display a Pin It button for websites on your content, I recommend the Pinterest "Pin It" Button plug-in. The Pinterest "Pin It" Button plug-in is a plug-in that only displays a sharing button for Pinterest.

✔ The Sharing Is Caring plug-in displays sharing buttons for multiple sites (such as Facebook, Twitter, and Google+) as well as a Pinterest button.

✔ The last plug-in I recommend is the Pinterest RSS Widget. This plug-in displays a widget with your most recent pins and a Follow Me on Pinterest button that's customizable.

If you currently have no sharing buttons for social networks, I recommend using the plug-in that adds several at one time. That way, you add the benefits of easy sharing on Pinterest as well as other popular social networks.

The Pinterest "Pin It" Button plug-in

The standalone Pin It button plug-in I recommend is the Pinterest "Pin It" Button plug-in. You can see details at `http://wordpress.org/extend/plugins/pinterest-pin-it-button` for the plug-in. (See Figure 10-14.)

Figure 10-14: The Pinterest "Pin It" Button plug-in.

To install this plug-in, follow these steps:

1. **Go to the dashboard of your WordPress site and log in.**

   The URL is typically `http://YOURDOMAIN.COM/wp-admin`.

2. **Under the Plugins menu, click Add New.**

   The Install Plugins page appears.

3. **In the Search Plugins text box, type** Pinterest Pin It Button **and then click the Search button. (See Figure 10-15.)**

   WordPress returns a list of results.

4. **Find the result for Pinterest "Pin It" Button and click the Install Now link.**

   A pop-up window appears and asks whether you're sure you want to install this plug-in.

5. **Click OK.**

   The Installing Plugin page appears and installs the plug-in on your site.

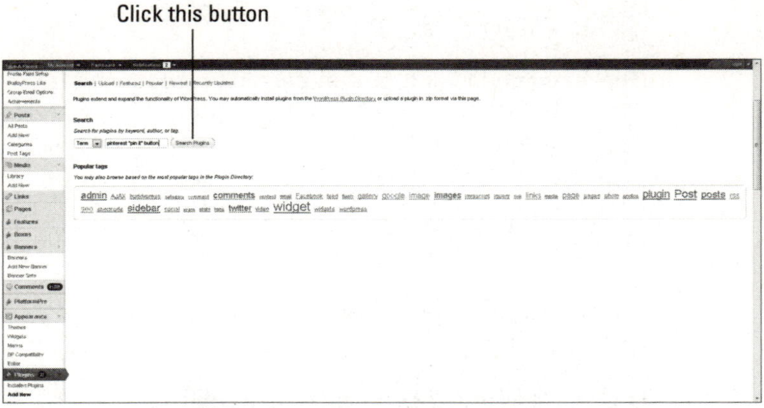

Click this button

Figure 10-15: Searching for the plug-in in your WordPress administration area.

6. **Click the Activate Plugin link to make the plug-in live on your site.**

   You return to your main Plugins page.

7. **Find the Pinterest "Pin It" Button option in your WordPress admin menu (usually in the left column or at the top of the page), and click it.**

   The Pinterest "Pin It" Button Settings page appears. From here you have a variety of options regarding where to display the button. You can choose the types of content as well as the physical location of the pin when it appears on content. (See Figure 10-16.)

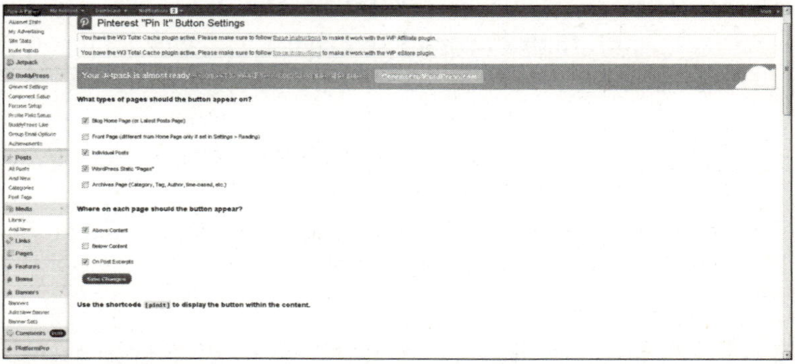

Figure 10-16: Setting your Pinterest "Pin It" Button preferences.

8. **Set your preferences and click the Save Changes button at the bottom of the page.**

9. **Visit your site as well as content types you selected the button to appear (such as pages or posts) to be sure it appears correctly.**

10. **Click the button to also be sure it works properly.**

 You can also use the short code `[pinit]` to display a pin anywhere manually in your content. This code can be handy for content with several images, where you want to remind people to pin right before or after images.

There is also a plug-in called Pin It on Pinterest, but in most instances I do not recommend it. With this plug-in, you must manually add a Pin It button to every post or page on your site one at a time (like you do with the standard Pin It web button code from Pinterest). Unless you have a very small site, this is cumbersome. It may be something to consider if you want more control over the image and description used in pins.

The Caring Is Sharing plug-in

The other Pin It plugin I recommend is the Sharing Is Caring plug-in. Although other social network sharing plug-ins are available, this one has a clean appearance, includes decent options, and works well.

To install the Sharing Is Caring plug-in, follow these steps:

1. **Go to the dashboard of your WordPress site and log in.**

   The URL is typically `http://YOURDOMAIN.COM/wp-admin`.

2. **Under the Plugins menu, click Add New.**

   The Install Plugins page appears.

3. **In the Search Plugins text box, type** Sharing Is Caring **and click the Search button.**

   WordPress returns a list of results.

4. **Find the result for Sharing Is Caring and click the Install Now link. (See Figure 10-17.)**

   A pop-up window appears and asks if you're sure you want to install this plug-in.

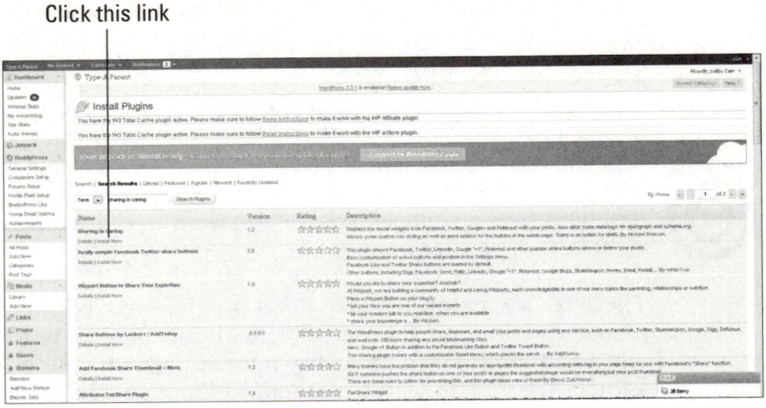

Click this link

Figure 10-17: Installing the Sharing Is Caring plug-in.

5. **Click OK.**

   The Installing Plugin page appears and installs the plug-in on your site.

6. **Click the Activate Plugin link. (See Figure 10-18.)**

   You return to the main Plugins page.

Click this link

Figure 10-18: Activating the Sharing Is Caring plug-in.

7. **From your WordPress admin menu (usually in the left column or at the top of the page), go to Settings and choose Sharing Is Caring from the menu.**

   The Sharing Is Caring settings page appears. The page offers you a variety of options regarding which social platform buttons to display and how to display them. You can also adjust the order and style of buttons as well as a variety of other minor settings. (See Figure 10-19.)

8. **Adjust the settings as you like and click the Save Changes button at the bottom of the page.**

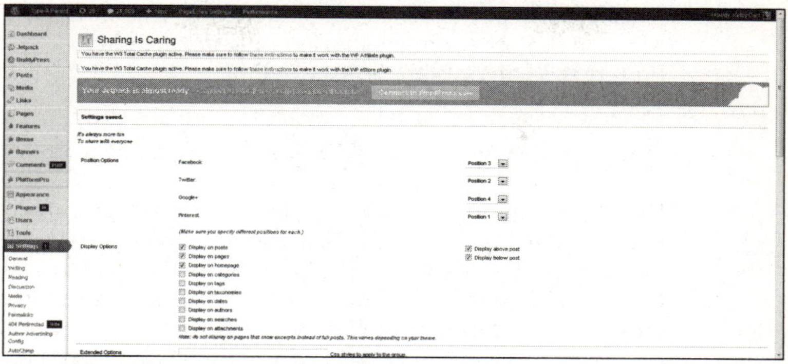

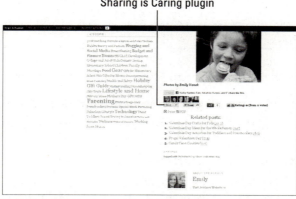

Figure 10-19: Setting your preferences in the Sharing Is Caring plug-in.

9. **View your website or blog and check any page types where the Sharing Is Caring button will be displayed to ensure it looks correct and doesn't interfere with your design.**

10. **Click the buttons to test and be sure they function properly.**

After you install the plug-in installed, you should have sharing icons for Pinterest, Twitter, Facebook, and Google+ (if all are enabled), and you can also display counts and recent people who liked the content on Facebook. (See Figure 10-20.)

Sharing is Caring plugin

Figure 10-20: The Sharing Is Caring plug-in in action.

There are a couple of other plug-ins that include multiple sharing buttons with Pinterest. They include Digg Digg, Slick Social Share Buttons, and Really Simple Facebook Twitter Share Buttons. Although I recommend Sharing Is Caring, you can also compare features or test the other plug-ins to find which one you prefer. Some of the other social sharing plug-ins are also likely to add Pinterest as an option soon as well.

The Pinterest RSS Widget

The third and final plug-in I recommend is the Pinterest RSS Widget plug-in. (See Figure 10-21.) This widget allows you to add a side-bar widget that displays your profile's recent pins and includes a Follow Me on Pinterest button at the bottom of the thumbnails (as shown on the left side of Figure 10-22).

Figure 10-21: The Pinterest RSS Widget plug-in page on WordPress.

To install the Pinterest RSS Widget, follow these steps:

1. **Go to the dashboard of your WordPress site and log in.**

   The URL is typically `http://YOURDOMAIN.COM/wp-admin`.

2. **Under the Plugins menu, click Add New.**

   The Install Plugins page appears.

3. **In the Search Plugins text box, type** Pinterest RSS Widget **and click the Search button.**

   WordPress returns a list of results.

Follow Me on Pinterest button

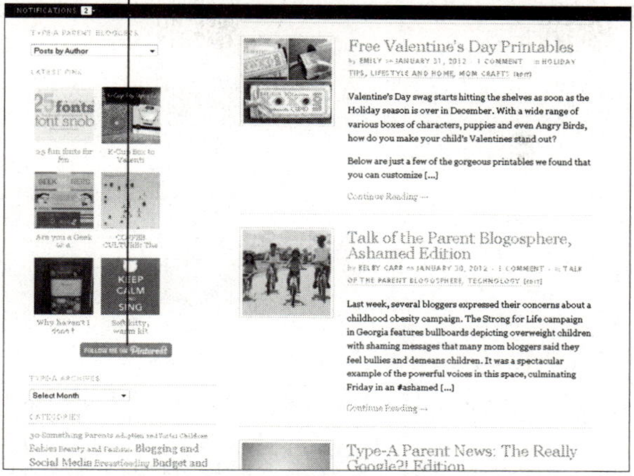

Figure 10-22: The Pinterest RSS Widget in a sidebar.

4. **Find the result for Pinterest RSS Widget and click the Install Now link.**

   A pop-up window appears and asks whether you're sure you want to install the plug-in.

5. **Click OK.**

   The Installing Plugin page appears and installs the plug-in on your site.

6. **Click the Activate Plugin link.**

   You return to the main plug-ins page.

7. **From your WordPress admin menu, go to Appearance and choose Widgets from the menu.**

   The Widgets page appears. Under the Available Widgets section, you'll now see Pinterest RSS Widget.

8. Click and drag Pinterest RSS Widget to the right to the sidebar where you want it to appear. (See Figure 10-23.)

9. **Click the down-pointing arrow to the right of the widget now placed in your sidebar.**

   You'll now see various options for the widget. (See Figure 10-24.)

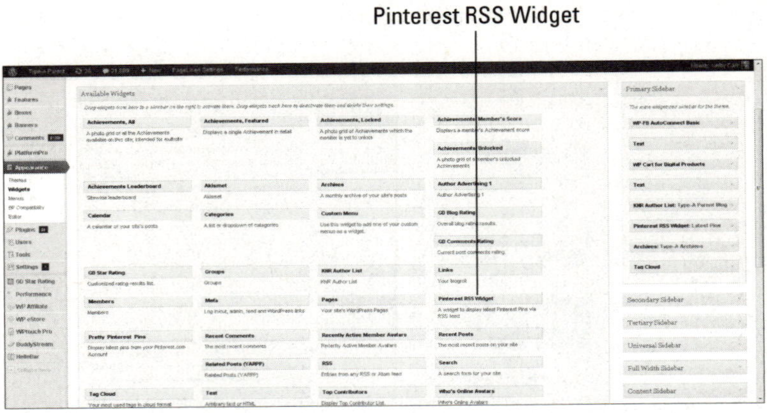

Pinterest RSS Widget

Figure 10-23: Placing the Pinterest RSS Widget in your sidebar.

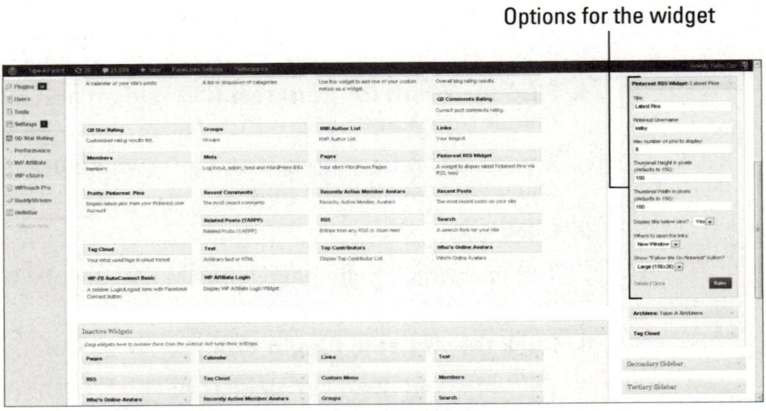

Options for the widget

Figure 10-24: Customizing the Pinterest RSS Widget.

10. **Complete each field.**

You can find your Pinterest username on your Pinterest profile URL after pinterest.com in the format `http://pinterest.com/USERNAME`.

11. **Click the Save button at the bottom of the widget settings box.**

12. **View your site to be sure the widget appears properly and click the Follow Me on Pinterest button to be sure it goes to your profile.**

There are also currently other Pinterest plug-ins for displaying your latest pins, so you can research, compare, and test those as well if you don't want the plug-in I recommend. They include Pinterest Pinboard Widget, Pretty Pinterest Pins, and Super Simple Pinterest Widget. More widget plug-ins are likely to be released soon as well.

Tracking Traffic Referrals from Pinterest

To gauge the effectiveness of Pinterest for driving traffic, you want to monitor your site's statistics to see how many visitors arrive from Pinterest. You can look at your site's referrals to see total traffic from Pinterest, and you can also dig into those referrals to determine which pins specifically drove a lot of traffic.

You can also compare Pinterest referrals with other popular sites for social sharing, such as Facebook and Twitter. You can examine how visitors from Pinterest behave when they arrive on your site and whether they stick around and visit other pages or they simply drop in and leave quickly.

There are quite a few site statistics programs, so it would be difficult to address them all here. I show how to find these statistics from two programs that I recommend: Google Analytics (which is free) and Get Clicky (which is free with limited features below 3,000 daily page views to your site or has a sliding pay scale if you get more traffic and want premium features). Even if you use another statistics program, any decent one includes data on referrals from other sites.

To track Pinterest effectiveness in Google Analytics, follow these steps:

1. **Log in to Google Analytics and select the site you want to examine and then the date range you want to view.**

2. **From the left menu, choose Traffic Sources➪Sources➪All Traffic.**

   The All Traffic page appears and shows you how Pinterest compares to all methods of entry to your site, as shown in Figure 10-25. If you have no Pinterest referrals yet, you will not see it in the list.

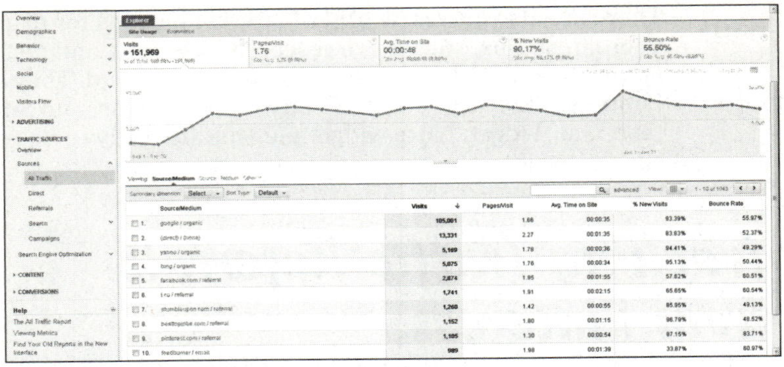

Figure 10-25: View all traffic in Google Analytics.

3. Also under Sources, click Referrals.

This step eliminates searches and direct site visits and shows you how Pinterest compares to other website referrals. (See Figure 10-26.) You can also view statistics to the right of each referring site on pages per visit, time on site, percentage that were new visitors to your site, and *bounce rate*. (A lower bounce rate is better than a higher bounce rate because it refers to the percentage of visitors who leave as soon as they arrive.)

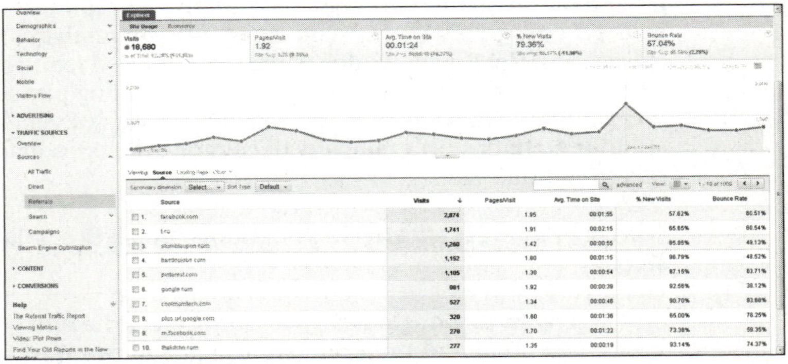

Figure 10-26: View all referrals in Google Analytics.

4. From this list, click Pinterest to see a page with a list of deep links on Pinterest that sent traffic to your site as well as total numbers on visitors from each pin. (See Figure 10-27.)

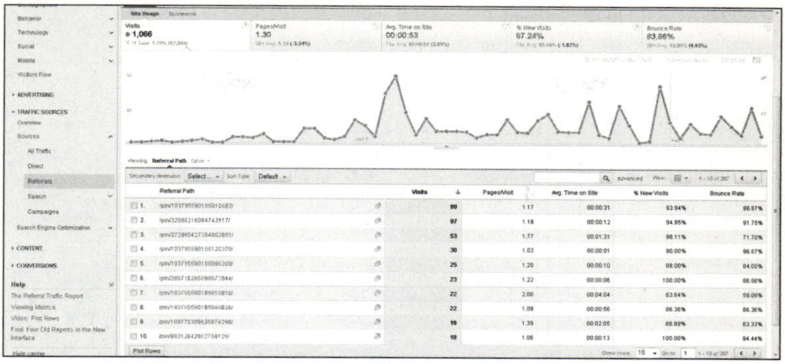

Figure 10-27: A list of deep links on Pinterest that drove traffic to your site.

5. **Click the arrow to the right of a URL in the list to go to the page on Pinterest and view it.**

   You can also click the URL itself in the list to get more details on that page as a referrer.

To track Pinterest referrals in Get Clicky, follow these steps:

1. **Log in to Get Clicky and navigate to the site you want to track.**

2. **At the top right, set the date range you want to view.**

3. **Halfway down the page on the left, look under the Links section.**

   You see all incoming links and the traffic totals. (See Figure 10-28.) This list shows you the deep links sending the most traffic.

4. **In the Links section, click Domains.**

   This shows a list of the domains sending the most traffic. (See Figure 10-29.)

5. **Click pinterest.com.**

   This step takes you to detailed statistics about visitors from the site as well as a comparison between Pinterest referred visitors and all other visitors when it comes to pages per visit, time on site, and bounce rate. If you have a premium account, you can also see the exact pins at the bottom of this screen and the number of referrals for each. Click the arrow to the right of a URL to go to the URL itself, or click the URL to see detailed stats about that inbound referral. (See Figure 10-30.)

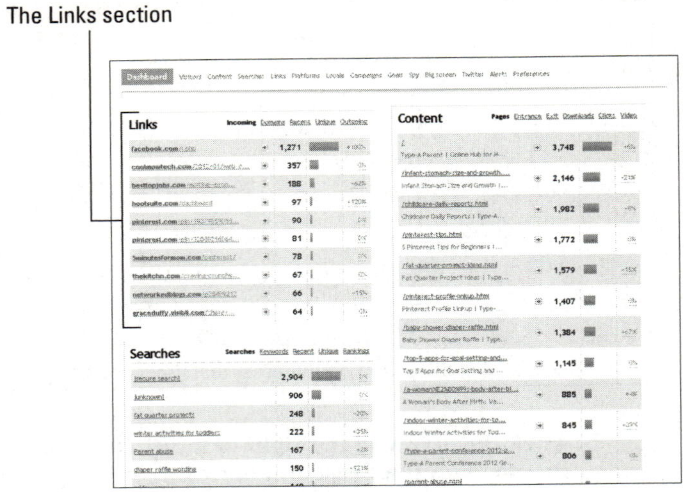

The Links section

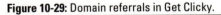

Figure 10-28: Incoming links in Get Clicky.

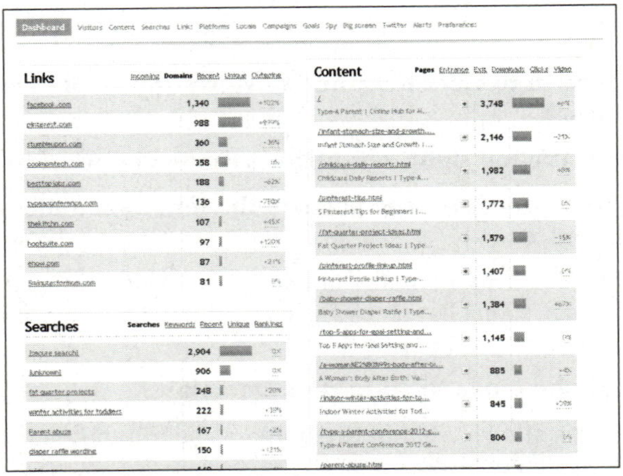

Figure 10-29: Domain referrals in Get Clicky.

Track statistics over time as you continue to use Pinterest to see how trends change. As you get more active on Pinterest and make your site more pin-friendly, you should see traffic from Pinterest increase.

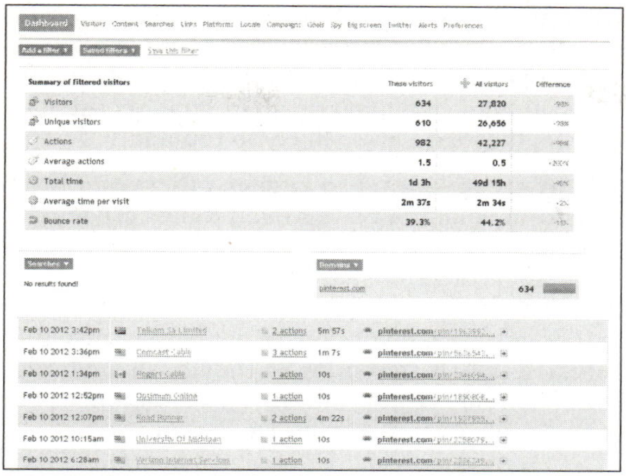

Figure 10-30: Detailed statistics on Pinterest referrals.

Using Pinterest to Engage Customers and Readers

If you're using Pinterest to draw readers or customers to your site, you want to be mindful of ways to engage them on Pinterest. Engaging users starts first and foremost with being an active and thoughtful participant of Pinterest. Beyond that, you want to consider what interests your audience and potential buyers.

Here are some tips for engaging readers and customers on Pinterest:

✔ **Be a good Pinterest citizen.** Be kind and thoughtful in your interactions with others and do your best to follow Pinterest etiquette. (Chapter 8 has more details on Pinterest etiquette.)

✔ **Be an active member.** Don't simply join and pin links to your site. Also, be sure to actively repin other members' pins and comment on others' pins.

✔ **Promote others first.** On social networks, people quickly forget those who only self-promote. They remember those who promoted them, however. Pin from other sites, especially in the same topic area that you cover on your own site.

✔ **Spread quality content.** One of the easiest ways to engage on Pinterest is to be a great pinner. Find content people will crave and enjoy, and they'll follow you more closely. They'll repin you. And when you do share that occasional link to your own site, they'll be more likely to repin it.

✔ **Look for creative ways to engage others on Pinterest.** Brainstorm what your site's main topics are and think of ways to spark interest and conversation among others on those topics. Also consider shared interests that your audience or customers might have, even if it isn't the exact topic of your site. For example, if your customers are moms, they aren't interested only in parenting — they're also interested in photography, home organization, and any number of other topics. Be part of the community conversation.

Chapter 11

Ten Companies Using Pinterest Effectively

Companies are increasingly becoming active on Pinterest, especially as the word gets out about its effectiveness to build awareness and traffic. Although some companies are just beginning to dabble on Pinterest, others are building large followings and sharing wonderful and interesting pins with their followers.

One issue worth noting is that many company pages tend to do a few things that I believe aren't terribly engaging or social: They follow very few people back, and a large portion of their pins link to their own content. Most people expect that from a company-specific profile, but in this chapter, I primarily highlight the companies that are following at least some people back, are sharing at least some content from sources outside their own site, have creative and engaging profiles, and are actively participating on Pinterest with a lot of pins and repins.

The Weather Channel

The Weather Channel does a good job of sharing what you would expect: straight weather-related content. You can browse boards that are creatively sparking interest and conversation in weather topics, and you can see that the company is having a bit of fun in its sharing. You can find the Weather Channel profile at `http://pinterest.com/weatherchannel`. (See Figure 11-1.)

Figure 11-1: The Weather Channel on Pinterest.

The Weather Channel boards include an iWitness Photos board where they pin their viewer-submitted photos, a board with pins for recipes for cold weather, a Weather Channel personalities board, and a board for space weather-related pins.

I like the originality, sharing of other sites' content, and unique topic for engaging fans of the Weather Channel with the Weather Style board at `http://pinterest.com/weatherchannel/weather-style`. (See Figure 11-2.)

Figure 11-2: The Weather Style board.

Cabot Cheese

The Cabot Cheese Pinterest presence impressed me in many ways. The company follows almost as many people as there are people following its profile. It freely shares others' content. It shows love to its home state through a <3 Vermont board, and it has a board dedicated to the farms and farmers who are part of its cheese cooperative.

The Cabot Cheese Pinterest profile also shares many recipes (and has several recipe boards), some of which are its own and some of which are from other sources. The recipes are interesting as pins, but the company also encourages people to buy and use its cheeses in their cooking. You can find the profile for Cabot Cheese at `http://pinterest.com/cabotcheese`. (See Figure 11-3.)

Figure 11-3: The Cabot Cheese Pinterest profile.

The folks at Cabot Cheese also aren't afraid to get silly on Pinterest, as you can see with the Moo! board at `http://pinterest.com/cabotcheese/moo`. (See Figure 11-4.)

Figure 11-4: The Moo! board.

Etsy

Much like the Etsy website, the Etsy Pinterest profile is full of beautiful things. I wish the folks working Etsy Pinterest shared more pins from other sites and followed more people, but they are active pinners, and their pins feature a lot of great products from various Etsy sellers. You can find Etsy on Pinterest at `http://pinterest.com/etsy`. (See Figure 11-5.)

Figure 11-5: Etsy on Pinterest.

Beyond sharing products by Etsy sellers, they also feature a recipe board and an Artsy Fartsy Board with several members pinning. They encourage others to be crafty with their DIY Projects board at `http://pinterest.com/etsy/diy-projects`. (See Figure 11-6.)

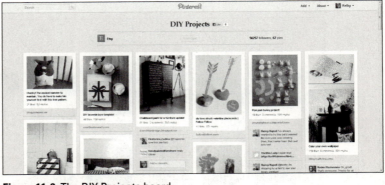

Figure 11-6: The DIY Projects board.

Lowe's

Lowe's is taking advantage of the popularity of home improvement and organization pins by having a presence on Pinterest. The Lowe's Pinterest account focuses on projects and crafts for the home. You can find Lowe's on Pinterest at `http://pinterest.com/lowes`. (See Figure 11-7.)

Figure 11-7: Lowe's on Pinterest.

The Lowe's boards include craft ideas, projects to make life easier for your pets, as well as a board dedicated to Lowe's home organization projects, Organize, at `http://pinterest.com/lowes/organize`. (See Figure 11-8.)

Figure 11-8: The Organize board.

TODAY

The *TODAY* show uses its Pinterest account to do a nice mix of self-promotion (that is still quite interesting) and content shared from around the web. *TODAY* can be found on Pinterest at `http://pinterest.com/todayshow`. (See Figure 11-9.)

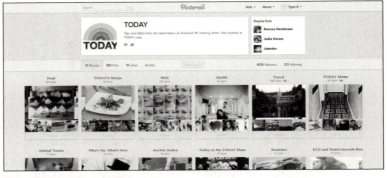

Figure 11-9: *Today* on Pinterest.

I love that the *TODAY* show shares some of its own great content (such as recipes from the show pinned to a *TODAY*'s Recipes board) but also has a lot of fun with its Pinterest profile. The Anchor Antics board shows the team goofing off. The Peacocks! board is filled with peacocks as well as images that are peacock-related, such as peacock eye shadow and shoes. The Peacocks! board can be found at `http://pinterest.com/todayshow/peacocks`. (See Figure 11-10.) It's a clever way to share the company's icon.

Figure 11-10: The Peacocks! board.

Scholastic

What stands out about the Scholastic Pinterest profile is that they have created fascinating boards that relate directly to their brand, but it also includes some fun and useful content related to its core topic of reading. You can follow Scholastic on Pinterest at `http://pinterest.com/scholastic`. (See Figure 11-11.)

Figure 11-11: Scholastic on Pinterest.

The company shares about Scholastic with boards such as Vintage Scholastic, which is sure to take you back in time, and Scholastic's Headquarters, with a mix of photos uploaded from behind the scenes at the Scholastic office as well as online content about the headquarters.

The folks at Scholastic also have several boards dedicated to the subject of reading in some way, such as creative bookcases, classroom ideas, and bling for bookworms. They feature some cool ideas on their Planning a Bookish Bash, such as book-themed party ideas, book-related cakes, and a book-exchange party idea. (See Figure 11-12.) You can find the board at `http://pinterest. com/scholastic/planning-a-bookish-bash`.

Whole Foods Market

Whole Foods Market shares a mix of recipes, kitchen gadgets, and tips on recycling and reusing. It also has several boards with multiple contributors. You can follow Whole Foods Market on Pinterest at `http://pinterest.com/wholefoods`. (See Figure 11-13.)

Figure 11-12: The Planning a Bookish Bash board.

Figure 11-13: Whole Foods Market on Pinterest.

One of the company's collaborative boards, How Does Your Garden Grow?, can be found at `http://pinterest.com/wholefoods/how-does-your-garden-grow`. (See Figure 11-14.) It includes a mix of gardening tips and infographics and sayings related to gardening and the organic lifestyle.

Real Simple

One of the earliest companies active on Pinterest, Real Simple uses its profile to share its diverse content on subjects such as cooking, fashion, organization, and family. I wish Real Simple followed more people and pinned from other sites on occasion (it almost never does), but it has a strong presence on Pinterest, its pinned content is interesting, and it has shared hundreds of pins. You can follow Real Simple at `http://pinterest.com/realsimple`. (See Figure 11-15.)

Figure 11-14: The How Does Your Garden Grow? board.

Figure 11-15: Real Simple on Pinterest.

The Real Simple boards cover a wide variety of topics, such as hairstyles, easy decorating ideas, and best slow cooker recipes. The company offers some ingenious ideas on its New Uses for Old Things board, which you can find at `http://pinterest.com/realsimple/new-uses-for-old-things`. (See Figure 11-16.)

Figure 11-16: The New Uses for Old Things board.

Better Homes and Gardens

The *Better Homes and Gardens* profile is packed with ideas on what
to cook, home décor, gardening, DIY projects, and parties. This is
another company that almost exclusively pins its own content, but
with dozens of boards and hundreds of pins, there's some incredible content here. You can follow *Better Homes and Gardens* on
Pinterest at `http://pinterest.com/bhg`. (See Figure 11-17.)

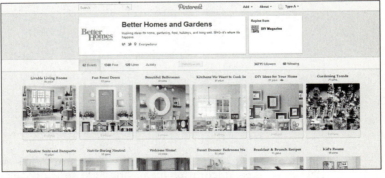

Figure 11-17: *Better Homes and Gardens* on Pinterest.

I love that the company engages with the online community of
bloggers by having boards such as Blogger Faves from BHG,
Blogger Twists on BHG Recipes, and Blogger Home Projects We
Love, which you can find at `http://pinterest.com/bhg/`
`blogger-home-projects-we-love`. (See Figure 11-18.)

Figure 11-18: The Blogger Home Projects We Love board.

Michaels Stores

The Michaels Stores Pinterest profile does a fabulous job sharing content of interest to its crafty audience on everything from baking and scrapbooking to weddings and holidays.

Because the Michaels website has so much related content you might think it pushes its own links heavily. However, it promotes great project tips and ideas from all over the web. It also follows back many of its followers. You can follow Michaels Stores on Pinterest at `http://pinterest.com/michaelsstores`. (See Figure 11-19.)

Figure 11-19: Michaels Stores on Pinterest

The company's most community-minded board is Projects from Followers, which features a diverse mix of pins of projects from people who follow them. You can follow the board at `http://pinterest.com/michaelsstores/projects-from-followers`. (See Figure 11-20.)

Figure 11-20: The Projects from Followers board.

More Companies on Pinterest

The preceding ten are obviously just a short list of standout companies on Pinterest. Many other companies and organizations are already active on Pinterest. Although it would be difficult to provide a comprehensive list, here are a few more interesting company profiles on Pinterest.

This tip might seem obvious, but don't forget to check out the Pinterest profile on Pinterest! You can find it at `http://pinterest.com/pinterest`.

If you're feeling hungry, the pinboards hosted by these companies will make you even more so:

- ✔ Betty Crocker, `http://pinterest.com/betty_crocker`
- ✔ Cooking Light, `http://pinterest.com/cookinglight`
- ✔ Epicurious, `http://pinterest.com/epicurious`
- ✔ Food Network, `http://pinterest.com/foodnetwork`
- ✔ Keurig, Inc., `http://pinterest.com/keuriginc`
- ✔ Kraft Recipes, `http://pinterest.com/kraftrecipes`
- ✔ Little Debbie, `http://pinterest.com/thelittledebbie`
- ✔ Lindt Chocolate, `http://pinterest.com/lindtchocolate`

- ✔ Pepperidge Farm Puff Pastry, `http://pinterest.com/PUFFPASTRY`
- ✔ Pillsbury, `http://pinterest.com/pillsburyideas`
- ✔ Williams-Sonoma, `http://pinterest.com/williamssonoma`

For a look at some fashion companies making a splash on Pinterest, try the following:

- ✔ Chobani, `http://pinterest.com/chobani`
- ✔ Gap, `http://pinterest.com/gap`
- ✔ Nordstrom, `http://pinterest.com/nordstrom`
- ✔ Kate Spade NY, `http://pinterest.com/katespadeny`

Some news channels, periodicals, and other media outlets are also getting in on the pin fun:

- ✔ *Lucky Magazine*, `http://pinterest.com/luckymagazine`
- ✔ *Newsweek*, `http://pinterest.com/newsweek`
- ✔ *Shape Magazine*, `http://pinterest.com/shapemagazine`
- ✔ *TIME*, `http://pinterest.com/time_magazine`
- ✔ Travel Channel, `http://pinterest.com/travelchannel`
- ✔ *The Wall Street Journal*, `http://pinterest.com/wsj`

And here are a few more miscellaneous companies:

- ✔ The American Association of Retired Persons, better known as AARP, has pinboards for all ages at `http://pinterest.com/aarp_official`.
- ✔ AMD, a tech company that makes computer components and processors, is at `http://pinterest.com/amdunprocessed`.
- ✔ Blockbuster, which rents movies and games, is at `http://pinterest.com/blockbuster`.
- ✔ Creative Memories, a scrapbooking company, is at `http://pinterest.com/creative_mems`.
- ✔ General Electric, one of the world's largest companies known for making everything from light bulbs to kitchen appliances, is at `http://pinterest.com/generalelectric`.
- ✔ HGTV, a home and garden cable TV network, is at `http://pinterest.com/hgtv`.

- ✔ Jo-Ann Fabric and Craft Stores, which sells sewing and craft supplies, is at `http://pinterest.com/joannstores`.

- ✔ Major League Baseball, the organization that represents United States baseball, is at `http://pinterest.com/mlbam`.

- ✔ Mashable, a popular blog covering the social media industry, is at `http://pinterest.com/mashable`.

- ✔ Melissa and Doug, a children's toy company, is at `http://pinterest.com/melissaanddoug`.

- ✔ National Wildlife Foundation, a nonprofit dedicated to preserving wild animals, is at `http://pinterest.com/nwfpins`.

- ✔ Oreck, a vacuum cleaner manufacturer, is at `http://pinterest.com/oreck`.

- ✔ Realtor.com, the U.S. organization for real estate agents, is at `http://pinterest.com/realtordotcom`.

Chapter 12

Ten Power Pinners to Follow

In This Chapter

▶ Ten powerful Pinterest members

▶ What makes these members worth following

*P*interest is said to have millions of members, but finding the great ones to follow can be a challenge. Sure, you can find members by integrating Facebook and following your friends who are on Pinterest. But what if you want to follow new people, ones you don't already know in real life or on other social networks?

I've created this list of ten power pinners, all people who are extremely active on Pinterest and who share incredible content. Because Pinterest doesn't offer any way to rank users by any sort of metrics, such as number of followers or number of pins, this isn't a *top* ten list — it's simply ten profiles that are interesting, active, and endorsed by way of thousands of followers each.

Another great way to find people to follow is through `http://spinterest.com`, a new site and app that's in beta/invitation-only stage at the time of this writing but should be public soon. It allows you to randomly spin through pins and click follow to follow members or boards as you do.

Michael Wurm

Michael Wurm is a Pennsylvania innkeeper, entrepreneur, artist, and self-proclaimed "wanna be designer" with more than 730,000 Pinterest followers. You can follow his profile at `http://pinterest.com/inspiredbycharm`. (See Figure 12-1.)

Figure 12-1: Michael Wurm on Pinterest.

His boards focus primarily on food and design, with several boards dedicated to one or the other. He has one board with great ideas and recipes for the first meal of the day, I Cook – Breakfast, that you can find at `http://pinterest.com/inspiredbycharm/ i-cook-breakfast/`. (See Figure 12-2.)

Figure 12-2: Michael Wurm's breakfast board.

Joy Cho

If you're joining Pinterest for all things pretty, Joy Cho is a must-follow member. A graphic designer, blogger at Oh Joy!, and foodie, her pins are quite simply beautiful. She primarily pins fashion, food, and art/design. You can follow Joy Cho at `http:// pinterest.com/ohjoy`. (See Figure 12-3.)

Figure 12-3: Joy Cho on Pinterest.

She has boards dedicated to graphic design, clothing, food, and dream homes. Some of her most unique pins are on her Quirky Little Things board, which you can follow at `http://pinterest.com/ohjoy/quirky-little-things`. (See Figure 12-4.)

Figure 12-4: Joy Cho's Quirky Little Things board.

Nester Smith

Nester Smith, known for her blog Nesting Place at `http://the nester.com`, has a pinboard filled with lovely images primarily dominated by home décor. She also pins content related to Pinterest, food, books, and crafts. You can follow her at `http://pinterest.com/nesters`. (See Figure 12-5.)

Figure 12-5: Nester Smith on Pinterest.

Her boards include I Don't Love This, with humorous pins of the bizarre and disturbing. She also has a board dedicated to home improvement and décor projects called Hackable, which you can find at `http://pinterest.com/nesters/hackable`. (See Figure 12-6.)

Figure 12-6: Nester Smith's Hackable board.

Jenny Lawson

Pinterest isn't just about the lovely, delicious, and inspirational. It's also a great site for getting a good laugh. There are few who nail the hilarious with better precision than humor blogger Jenny Lawson, also known as The Bloggess. You can follow her at `http://pinterest.com/thebloggess/`. (See Figure 12-7.)

Figure 12-7: Jenny Lawson on Pinterest.

Her pins are a manic mix of tattoos and irreverent quotes (some-times featuring expletives) with an occasional zombie thrown in for good measure. Her most active board, with almost 40,000 fol-lowers, is Kick-A** Stuff. (See Figure 12-8.)

Figure 12-8: Jenny Lawson's Kick-A** board.

Marine Loiseau

With an emphasis on the attractive and a dash of the quirky, the Marine Loiseau stream of pins has something interesting for most people. A tattoo board is sandwiched between a work board and a board featuring attractive celebrities. You can follow Luce de Luce at http://pinterest.com/lucedeluce. (See Figure 12-9.)

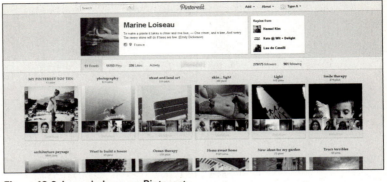

Figure 12-9: Luce de Luce on Pinterest.

The boards include a few dedicated to photography and various colors, as well as a Nature Inside board with some clever ideas for bringing the outside into your home. You can follow the Nature Island board at `http://pinterest.com/lucedeluce/nature-inside`. (See Figure 12-10.)

Figure 12-10: Luce de Luce's Nature Inside board.

Steven McGaughey

Steven McGaughey, a medical student with a passion for design, has a great mix of pins that include some topics that are less frequently pinned, such as travel gear, building a bicycle, and logos. You can follow Steven McGaughey at `http://pinterest.com/stevenm`. (See Figure 12-11.)

Figure 12-11: Stephen McGaughey on Pinterest.

He has boards dedicated to his favorite iPhone apps, architecture, and cool products. His All Lit Up board includes unique light fixtures and lamps and can be followed at `http://pinterest. com/stevenm/all-lit-up`. (See Figure 12-12.)

Figure 12-12: Steven McGaughey's All Lit Up board.

Amy Clark

Amy Clark of the blog Mom Advice shares a wide variety of pins on everything from photography and food to upcycling and organizing. You can follow her at `http://pinterest.com/mom advice/`. (See Figure 12-13.)

Figure 12-13: Amy Clark on Pinterest.

Her board, Being the Cool Mom, includes pins related to fun and creative things to do with children such as creating a killer paper airplane and fun ideas for movie-time snacks. You can follow the board at `http://pinterest.com/momadvice/being-the-cool-mom/`. (See Figure 12-14.)

Figure 12-14: Amy Clark's Being the Cool Mom board.

Jaden Hair

Jaden Hair is a food blogger at Steamy Kitchen, a television chef on Daytime, and a food columnist for Discovery Health, TLC, and Tampa Tribune. You can follow her at `http://pinterest.com/steamykitchen/`. (See Figure 12-15.)

Figure 12-15: Jaden Hair on Pinterest.

Her boards include fashion, home décor, travel and crafts. She has a few boards dedicated to cooking and food, such as Recipes to Savor 'n Sip. You can follow that board at `http://pinterest.com/steamykitchen/recipes-to-savor-n-sip/`. (See Figure 12-16.)

Figure 12-16: Jaden Hair's Recipes to Savor 'n Sip board.

Heather Mann

If crafting is your passion, Heather Mann is a must-follow. The founder of Dollar Store Crafts and Craft Fail blogs, she pins a wide variety of craft projects and ideas. You can follow her at `http://pinterest.com/heathermann1/`. (See Figure 12-17.)

Figure 12-17: Heather Mann on Pinterest.

Her boards include a wide variety of topics beyond crafting, such as a geek board, an Oregon board, and a blogging tips board. To see the best of her craft finds, though, follow her Crafty board at `http://pinterest.com/heathermann1/crafty/`. (See Figure 12-18.)

Figure 12-18: Heather Mann's Crafty board.

Sfgirlbybay

Sfgirlbybay's Pinterest account is a great one to follow for cool products, with an emphasis on gorgeous style and a hint of geek chic. She shares home design, kitchen gadgets, and funky furniture. You can follow Sfgirlbybay at `http://pinterest.com/sfgirl bybay`. (See Figure 12-19.)

Figure 12-19: Sfgirlbybay on Pinterest.

Her boards include Surf Style, Four Eyes, and Geek Love, which you can follow at `http://pinterest.com/sfgirlbybay/ geek-love`. (See Figure 12-20.)

Figure 12-20: Sfgirlbybay's Geek Love board.

More Power Pinners to Consider Following

Here are a few more great pinners to follow:

- ✔ Patricia van Essche at `http://pinterest.com/pvedesign` for design and art

- ✔ Julie (Angry Julie) at `http://pinterest.com/angryjulie` for photography

- ✔ Audrey McClellan at `http://pinterest.com/audrey mcclellan` for fashion

- ✔ Justin and Cassidy at `http://pinterest.com/remodel aholic` for home DIY

- ✔ Robin Plemmons at `http://pinterest.com/robin plemmons` for irreverent humor and crafts

- ✔ Serious Eats at `http://pinterest.com/seriouseats` for great food pins

- ✔ Scott Stratten at `http://pinterest.com/unmarketing` for the quirky

- ✔ Sarah of Thrifty Décor Chick at `http://pinterest.com/ thriftydecor` for inexpensive décor ideas

Index